Francis Cuthbert Doyle

The life of Gregory Lopez

Francis Cuthbert Doyle

The life of Gregory Lopez

ISBN/EAN: 9783742835925

Manufactured in Europe, USA, Canada, Australia, Japa

Cover: Foto ©Andreas Hilbeck / pixelio.de

Manufactured and distributed by brebook publishing software (www.brebook.com)

Francis Cuthbert Doyle

The life of Gregory Lopez

THE LIFE
OF
GREGORY LOPEZ.

BY
CANON DOYLE, O.S.B.

Fiat voluntas tua, sicut in cœlo, et in terra. Amen. Jesus.

LONDON:
R. WASHBOURNE, 18 PATERNOSTER ROW.
1876.

✠

SANCTISSIMO JOSEPH,

BEATISSIMÆ SEMPERQUE VIRGINIS MARIÆ, SPONSO,

ET

UNIVERSALIS ECCLESIÆ PATRONO,

HOC OPUSCULUM

CORDE AMANTISSIMO

𝕯𝖎𝖈𝖆𝖙

AUCTOR.

PREFACE.

IT was during a summer evening's ramble, many years ago, that I first heard from the lips of a dear friend, the story of Gregory Lopez. Meagre and imperfect as that account was necessarily obliged to be, it nevertheless gave me a desire to learn still more about a life so extraordinary and so holy. Up to that moment I had known little more of Gregory than the name, and some few isolated facts, such as are to be found scattered here and there in the pages of spiritual books. I was glad, therefore, to hear that there was extant an authentic account of his life and actions. For my friend, while searching through the shelves of one of our monastic libraries, had come upon the few tattered leaves from which he had gleaned the facts which he imparted to me.

It was not, however, till several years after, that good fortune threw in my way, a copy of a work which must now be very rare. A gentleman, who was on very friendly terms with one of our Fathers, chanced, while passing a bookstall in one of our provincial towns, to catch a glimpse of the seal of one of our monasteries upon the title-page of a small volume, which was in a rather dilapidated condition. He examined the book, found it to be a life of Gregory Lopez, and at the expense of a few coppers, rescued it from the waste-paper basket. He presented it to the Father, as a curiosity, and from his hands I received that for which I had searched in vain for so long a time.

It appears from the title-page, that it "was done out of Spanish," in the year 1675, and evidently by a not very skilful hand. The original was written by Father Losa, and published in 1612. It consists of a lengthy dissertation upon Gregory, followed by the narrative of his life, together with several approbations from Bishops and Doctors of Divinity, couched in terms of the very highest admiration and praise.

After carefully selecting all the chief facts of Gregory's life, from the narrative of Father Losa, I have thrown them,—together with matter from other sources,—into their present form, with a view to encourage, by the example of a most blameless life, those who are striving to cultivate in their hearts a spirit of affective prayer, of self-denial, and of humble resignation to the Holy Will of God; and also to prevent the memory of a good man from perishing off the face of the earth.

F. C. D.

St. Michael's Priory, Hereford,
    Feast of St. Augustine,
        May 26th, 1876.

PROTESTATIO.

JUXTA SS. D. N. Urbani Papæ VIII Decretum, die 13 Martii 1625, editum, profiteor me haud alio sensu, quidquid in hoc libro refero, accipere, aut accipi ab ullo velle, quàm quo ea solent, quæ humana dumtaxat auctoritate, non autem Divina Catholicæ Romanæ Ecclesiæ, aut Sanctæ Sedis Apostolicæ, nituntur. Iis tantummodo exceptis, quos eadem Sancta Sedes, Sanctorum, Beatorum, aut Martyrum Catalogo adscripsit.

CONTENTS.

PART I.

CHAP.		PAGE
I.	FROM HIS BIRTH TILL HIS DEPARTURE FOR NEW SPAIN	1
II.	THE BEGINNING OF HIS SOLITARY LIFE	10
III.	HIS TEMPTATIONS AND THEIR REMEDIES	19
IV.	GREGORY LEAVES HIS SOLITUDE, AND GOES TO MEXICO	23
V.	HIS RETURN TO THE SOLITARY LIFE	31
VI.	HIS TRIALS	34
VII.	GREGORY RETIRES TO ATRISCO, AND TO THE SANCTUARY OF OUR LADY OF REMEDIES	39
VIII.	GREGORY REMOVES TO THE HOSPITAL OF GUASTECA	49
IX.	SICKNESS COMPELS GREGORY TO GO TO MEXICO, AND THENCE TO SANTA FÉ	56
X.	GREGORY'S LIFE AND DAILY EXERCISES AT SANTA FÉ	60
XI.	HIS LAST ILLNESS AND DEATH	68
XII.	SIGNS IN EVIDENCE OF GREGORY'S SANCTITY	81
XIII.	MIRACLES WORKED BY GREGORY'S RELICS	85

PART II.

I.	HIS KNOWLEDGE OF SACRED SCRIPTURE	93
II.	HIS SPIRITUAL DISCERNMENT	98
III.	HIS KNOWLEDGE OF HISTORY, SACRED AND PROFANE	112

CONTENTS.

CHAP.		PAGE
IV.	HIS KNOWLEDGE OF OTHER SCIENCES	118
V.	GOVERNMENT OF THE TONGUE	123
VI.	HIS WISDOM IN WORD AND WORK	132
VII.	HIS COURAGE AND MAGNANIMITY	140
VIII.	HIS HUMILITY AND INTERIOR POVERTY	152
IX.	HIS EXTERNAL POVERTY	159
X.	MORTIFICATIONS AND SUFFERINGS	167
XI.	MORTIFICATION OF THE SENSES	180
XII.	HIS SPIRIT OF PRAYER	187
XIII.	HIS PRAYER IN SOLITUDE	191
XIV.	ANSWERS GIVEN BY GREGORY, WHICH MANIFEST HIS SPIRIT	197
XV.	OTHER KINDS OF PRAYER USED BY GREGORY LOPEZ	202
XVI.	HIS ABIDING UNION WITH GOD	211
XVII.	THE EFFECTS OF HIS PRAYER	218
XVIII.	REVERENCE EXCITED BY HIS APPEARANCE	226

THE LIFE OF GREGORY LOPEZ.

CHAPTER I.

FROM HIS BIRTH TILL HIS DEPARTURE FOR NEW SPAIN.

THE wonderful man, whose life shall occupy the following pages, was born at Madrid, in the year 1542, and on the feast day of St. Gregory Thaumaturgus, which at that time was celebrated on the fourth of July. He was called Gregory after the Saint upon whose festival he was born; but Lopez is generally supposed to have been a name which he assumed. Of his parents and family scarcely anything is known. He never mentioned them, nor could any information respecting them, or the position they held in society, ever be extracted from him by the most adroit and pointed questioning. All that could be gathered from the little he did say, was that he was the youngest of a considerably large family, which consisted of two girls and several boys. We may judge how completely he had severed himself from all ties of flesh and blood, from the fact that during the four and thirty years he lived in New Spain, he never once communicated with any of his relatives.

His complete silence about all such matters naturally enough set the curious conjecturing and puzzling their heads to discover his secret, for secret they decided he most certainly had, or he would never so studiously fence himself round with mystery.

Many rumours were consequently set on foot about him, the latest, as is usual in such cases, contradicting the one that had immediately preceded it; but that which seemed to meet with the most general favour from the public, was to the effect that he was some great and illustrious personage, who, for reasons of his own, or perhaps through love of humility, had thrown aside his worldly rank, and chosen to spend his days in this new world, undistinguished and unknown. Some support was needed to give at least an air of probability to their conjecture; so the wise ones would nod significantly, and call attention to the inbred dignity of his behaviour when treating with persons of the highest rank, as proof positive that Gregory was the scion of some great and noble house.

Whether this were true or not, we shall never know; but certain it is that he possessed the courtly polish which the eager, prying eyes of idle gossips detected in him; for while preserving a humble gravity of demeanour in the company of the great, he was yet perfectly at ease and self-possessed. To the questions they put to him, he answered with that freedom from embarrassment, and that grace of mien, which are acquired only by moving in the higher circles of society.

The priest, from whose narrative the materials for the present life of Gregory are taken, was curious, like the rest, to learn something of his parentage. Trusting, therefore, to the close terms of intimacy on which he lived with the holy man, he one day took the liberty to ask Gregory himself some very pertinent questions on this point. But even these elicited nothing, except that his family was rather poor than rich. Their name, however, never transpired. When asked to reveal it, a few days before his death, he said very quietly: "Since I entered upon this manner of life, I have ever looked upon God as my Father; as for my brothers, they must all be dead by this time, for I was the youngest." We may see from this how little value he attached to nobility of birth. Some pride themselves upon it so much, that they imagine it will serve them instead of intellect, or even of that truer nobility which has the patent of the Great King to vouch for its authenticity—a virtuous life, full of beautiful thoughts, and high aspirations, and noble, sterling actions. With such nobility as this, God seems to have invested him at a very early age; for when questioned as to the precise time when he had first begun to serve God, he said that he was not quite sure if it was when he attained the use of reason, but that it must have been very soon after that time.

As a matter of fact, he had never been childish in his manners; in malice only he had ever been a veritable child. Hence he used frequently to repeat the words of Jeremias, as if he had had a practical experience of their truth: "It is a good thing for a man to have borne the yoke from his youth."

The education which he received seems to have been most rudimentary in its character, and was probably such as would be given at the present day in schools of the humblest class. He never studied what are called "the classical languages," so that we may ascribe his after knowledge of them to the infused light he received from the Holy Spirit, Who at times bestows in a moment what the keenest intellects can acquire only after years of persevering study.

While he was yet a mere child, he is said to have left home, without the knowledge of his parents, and to have travelled on till he came into the kingdom of Navarre. There he met with a pious solitary, with whom he took up his abode. Under his guidance he remained for six years, and was trained by him in all the duties and exercises of a religious life. This abandonment of home will doubtless seem to many, anything but a holy and religious action. It will be looked upon by them rather as an indication of that want of filial affection reprobated by St. Paul. But before we dare to pass judgment upon holy men, we must bear in mind that God does not draw them to Himself by the ordinary laws whereby He guides the great mass of Christians; for, since He intends them to be exceptionally great in the way of virtue, He leads them by exceptional paths, and inspires them to do exceptional deeds, which ought not to prove stumbling-blocks to those who are travelling along the ordinary beaten track. In their extraordinary and wonderful actions, God wishes us to admire, but not to imitate them. St. John the Baptist "was in the desert until the day of his manifestation to Israel." Our holy Father, St. Benedict, left his home at the age of thirteen, and lived a hermit's life. Our Lord Himself left His parents when a child, and remained behind them in Jerusalem, occupied with the affairs of His heavenly Father's kingdom. We may presume, therefore, to say that Gregory was led by the Spirit of God into solitude, that his heart might be inflamed with holy desires, and the seeds of future virtues planted therein, to spring up and bear fruit for his support in that life of utter self-abnegation which he was afterwards to lead.

His parents were naturally enough alarmed, and exceedingly grieved at his sudden disappearance. Like that ever blessed couple, to whom the eternal, incarnate God disdained not to intrust Himself, they sought him sorrowing. Long and wearisome was their search. Their hearts grew sick with hope deferred, their eyes grew dim with bitter tears; but still they hoped on, and put their trust in God. Their patient, persevering search was at length rewarded with success. They found the joy of their hearts, and, drying their tears, bore him back exulting, "because he had been lost and was found; he had been to them as one dead, and behold he lived again."

Gregory was taken by his parents to Valladolid, where at this time the court resided. Much against his will, they had him placed as page, either to serve royalty itself, or some of the numerous grandees attendant upon the royal person.

Of these facts there is no further testimony than that of the Spanish author of his life, who says that he had them, and also the circumstance of his early life of solitude "from a person of great credit." Gregory himself told him that in early life he had lived at Burgos, which lies on the road from Madrid to Navarre, and that he had served as page at court. He also assured him that all the bustle of that princely residence, with its gaily-dressed ladies, its cavaliers, its soldiers, its pomp, and pride, and circumstance, could never for a moment make him forget God, or trouble that inward calm or recollection, to the practice of which his Lord was calling him. We find no difficulty, therefore, in readily believing him when he states, that while performing the ordinary duties of his position, his soul was ever occupied in holding sweetest converse with his God.

Before taking the decided step which was to shape the whole career of his future life, he resolved to make a pilgrimage to the shrine of our Lady of Guadalupe, which was then famous, not only in Spain, but also throughout the whole Catholic world. He accordingly set out upon his journey, and in due time arrived at the town which had grown up round the Monastery of the Hieronomite Monks, under whose care the Sanctuary had been placed by Don John I. in the year 1389. As he wended his way through its narrow, tortuous streets, his eye fell upon the frowning bastions and castellated walls of what seemed to be a superb citadel. Rampart and ditch and palisade spoke to him of a feudal stronghold capable of making a stout defence, and standing unmoved like a solid rock, amid the surging tide of war. Yet all within spoke of peace and charity. No sentinel stood at the open gate to check the entrance of the devout throng which passed incessantly across the lowered drawbridge; no man-at-arms looked from the watch-tower; no well drilled troop made the court within re-echo beneath their steady tramp. Only a few hooded monks swept across the open space, with downcast eye, and solemn gait. The time had passed away when all these warlike surroundings were of any use. They now served only to tell in their own mute way, of the troublesome times long gone by, in which life and property were so insecure, that he who would hold his possessions in peace, was obliged to be both able, and ready, and willing to defend them sword in hand, and at the peril of his life. Gregory soon discovered that this fortress-like structure, which looked to him so little like the abode of peaceful monks, was the protecting shield which the devout children of Mary had deemed necessary in bygone times to guard her shrine from the violence of impious marauders. Entering therefore with the crowd of pilgrims, he soon stood in the spacious church designed by the celebrated architect John Alphonso, and gazed with wonder upon the walls which spoke to him so eloquently in votive offerings of silver and of gold, in rich tapestry and valuable paintings, of the three thousand

authenticated miracles worked in favour of her devout
clients by the Mother of God. Then casting himself
upon his knees before her sacred image, round which the
brilliant light from a hundred silver lamps poured the
radiance of the noonday, he thought of the long ages
that had passed since the Christians of the fourth
century had bowed with reverence before it; he
thought of the love which must have burned in the
heart of that illustrious Pontiff, Gregory the Great, for
their own illustrious bishop St. Leander of Seville, when
he did not hesitate to deprive Italy of this treasure, that
he might testify unto him the affection of his heart. He
thought too of those evil days which fell upon Spain in
the first decade of the eighth century, when the Arabs of
the desert burst in upon her, and sweeping aside the
stalwart warriors of the Gothic King Roderic, poured
the invading flood of their savage hordes over her fruitful plains, to waste and to destroy. Then he remembered
how loving hands had taken this precious treasure and
hidden it together with the body of St. Fulgentius in
the cave of Guadalupe, hoping that the storm would
speedily pass away, and that they would soon be able to
bring it forth again for the veneration of the Faithful.
But God had decreed otherwise. The Moorish sway
lasted so long, that the hiding place of the statue was
forgotten, and its very existence unknown. Six long
centuries rolled away, and then a humble shepherd was
chosen by God to be the instrument of its restoration to
the devout children of His blessed Mother. And now,
for more than two hundred years, the Faithful had been

flocking to the shrine which royal munificence had raised for her, and not a few had experienced that the power of her intercession with God was as efficacious, and even more so, than when she whispered in His ear at the marriage feast of Cana: " Son, they have no wine !" All these thoughts flashed through his mind as he knelt there and poured forth his heart in prayer throughout the silent hours of the night, beseeching the Virgin of virgins, the guide of pilgrims, to obtain for him from her divine Son, light to know whither he should direct his steps to serve God with greatest profit, both to himself and to his neighbour. At length he received an internal answer to his prayer, which bade him go to Mexico, or New Spain as it was then called, and the conviction came upon him, that there it would be told him what he was to do. Upon another occasion, while kneeling in prayer in the great church of Toledo, Almighty God seems to have poured a flood of light into his soul, concerning the manner of life he was to lead in the new world; but whether this favour was granted to him before, or after his pilgrimage to Guadalupe, we have never been able accurately to determine. It seems to have been a grace of so extraordinary a nature, that Gregory himself frequently declared, that he had never before experienced the like.

This is all that can be learnt about the life which he led up to his twentieth year. It was a life, rich, no doubt, in the practice of all those good works which are the fruit of the Holy Spirit's abiding presence in the soul. But what they were, we know not. They are hidden with Christ in God. No human eye shall look upon them until the great accounting day, when God shall manifest them before angels and men, that His faithful servant may receive the commendation and glory due to them.

CHAPTER II.

THE BEGINNING OF HIS SOLITARY LIFE.

IT was no vulgar greed for gold which led Gregory from his own country to the coast of New Spain. The inward promptings of the Holy Spirit bade him go forth from his father's house, from his country and his kindred, and betake himself to the land which should be shown him. With humble obedience, and a faith, firm as that of the Patriarch of old, he yielded to the mandate of God, and turning his back upon all that was dear to him, "retired into solitude that the Lord might speak to his heart."

But first, he had to bear all the fatigues, and experience all the discomforts which are the lot of those "who go down to the sea in ships." These are bad enough in our own day, when modern refinement has gathered round itself every species of luxurious comfort, and modern ingenuity has devised means and appliances whereby the ills of life may be so smoothed and softened as to become almost imperceptible. Three centuries ago they must have been very considerable, and we may take it for granted that Gregory, in his eagerness for mortification, had more than his due share of them. Bad as they were, like most temporal evils, they came to an end when the vessel dropped her anchor in the port of St. John de Ulloa.

Her passengers speedily disembarked, being only too glad to escape from the cramped and crowded decks of the ship, and tread once more upon the firm earth, which to most of them was a new land, full of the bright promises of a golden future. Without betraying any of that emotion, so pardonable in one who, after a long and perilous voyage, opens his eye for the first time upon a new world, Gregory also made his way to the boats which conveyed the passengers to the shore, and was soon landed in the town of Vera Cruz.

It must then have been little better than a straggling sort of village, for the present town was not built until the latter part of the sixteenth century; yet, even at the time of which we write, Philip III. had conferred upon it the title as well as the privileges of a city, influenced no doubt by the excellence of its position, which has since made it one of the great centres of commerce between the Old and the New World.

But though so admirably situated, from a mercantile point of view, its position, upon one of those marshy flats which border the Gulf of Mexico, make it a very charnel-house at certain seasons of the year. The scourge of yellow-fever is domesticated there, and a glance at the barren sandhills and stagnant pools of water which lie beyond the city will account in great measure for the abiding presence there of this minister of death.

It was here that Gregory chose to put in practice the counsel given by Christ to the young man, who asked Him what he was to do to gain everlasting life,—he sold all that he possessed, realizing thereby about eight hundred crowns, which he distributed to the poor. When thus stripped of earthly possessions, he turned his face towards the great city of Mexico. His stay there was very short; in fact, he remained in it just long enough to gain by his penmanship a sufficient sum of money to carry him to the mining district of Zacatecas. He betook himself to this place, because he hoped to find there, what he had failed to discover in the environs of a great city,—a solitude where he might speak to his God, undisturbed by the noise of the busy world. That Mexico was the first place visited by him after quitting Vera Cruz, is clearly established by a letter which he received while residing at Santa-Fé. This came from a man named Louis Zapata, who, hearing of Gregory's wonderful life, wished to find out if he were the same person whom he had known in former years. It bears the date 1591, and is to the following effect: "Twenty-nine or thirty years ago, when I was dwelling in the street of Tacuba, in the city of Mexico, a gentleman came from Spain and lodged in my house. He was clad in serge, and during the entire Lent fasted most rigorously on bread and water. He was called Gregory Lopez. Hearing that you bear the same name, I beg of you to let me know if you are the same person. Commend me to God!"

The answer sent by Gregory is characteristic. It was written on the same sheet of paper and ran thus:—" I am the man you speak of, and will comply with your request." A very short residence at Zacatecas served to convince him, that it was as little suited for the abode of a solitary as Mexico itself. The "sacred thirst of gold" had drawn thither from every part of the Spanish colonies great numbers of men, whose sole aim was to amass a colossal fortune in the shortest possible time. Not a few of them were ready to employ very questionable means for this purpose, and many actually did so when an occasion offered itself, as the history of that period will amply testify. Gregory was sighing after treasures of a very different nature, which his quick eye told him could not be found there. Accordingly, after staying a few days, he determined to push on further into the country and leave behind him the haunts of greedy, self-seeking men. His departure was hastened by an incident of which he was an eye-witness. It chanced that as he was walking on the great Piazza, the waggons laden with silver were drawn up, and got in readiness to start for Mexico. This, though an event of ordinary occurrence, always attracted great crowds of people, made up, as crowds in such localities usually are, of a considerable number of very indifferent characters. There were there, adventurers, spendthrifts, and desperadoes,—men who had nothing to lose, who carried their lives in their hands, and cared little about exposing them to extreme peril. Some trifle or other gave rise to a few angry words between two of the bystanders; these speedily developed into threatening and abusive language, and ended in a heated altercation, during which a blow was struck. On the instant, out flashed their too ready swords. They fought with great fury for a few moments and fell, both mortally wounded. In fact, they died there on the spot where they fell. The sight of those two pale, blood-stained men, lying there with their last outburst of ungovernable rage stamped upon their features, was for Gregory a warning to flee from the society of those who were so forgetful of God and of themselves, as to risk eternal damnation for a mere word of contempt. It filled him with the most profound horror, and gave new force to the impulse of the Holy Spirit Who was so sweetly drawing him away into the desert places. Turning his back upon the scene of blood, he hastened with all speed from the district of Zacatecas, and sped onward into the country, for the distance of about twenty-five miles, till he came to the Valley of Amayac. Seeing that this place was admirably suited for one who wished to lead a solitary life, he determined to halt there. This valley was close upon the borders of the Chichimecos, who were at that time the most cruel and inveterate foes of the Spanish colonists. Gregory, however, had not the slightest fear of them. He was rather glad than otherwise, to be near them, that he might, if God so pleased, become an instrument in His Almighty hands, for bringing them to the fold of Christ. His first care then, was to build himself a little hut or hermitage, which was probably the first erected in the recently conquered country. The Indians soon discovered him, but made no attempt to do him any mischief. They gathered round him, and by a species of instinct, appeared to know that he was a man wholly devoted to the service of the Great Spirit. A kind of religious reverence seemed to take possession of them as they watched him, with great curiosity, while he was engaged in the building of his little abode. At length one, and then another and another, with every demonstration of respect and reverence, came forward and began to assist him in his work, so that his hermitage was speedily constructed. Gregory was barely twenty-one years old when he first entered upon this solitary way of life. Great indeed must have been his virtue, and evident the call of God. For one whose authority no one will call in question, is ot opinion, that those only who have fought long and well under the guidance of an experienced and skilful master, ought to attempt it. " Hermits," says our holy Father, St. Benedict, " are men who have learnt, not from any first fervour of devotion, but by long probation in the monastic life, and by the comfort and encouragement of others, to fight against the devil, and being now well armed, and secure even without the help of others, are able by God's assistance to strive hand to hand against the flesh and evil thoughts, and so go forth from the army of the brotherhood to the single combat of the wilderness." Gregory must have felt within himself a consciousness of being able to cope with the adversaries, which in solitude, gather round men such as he. He did not thrust himself into it with a presumptuous confidence in his own strength, but casting himself upon his knees in the sight of God, he said unto Him with childlike humility: "Oh Lord, I go forth from the company of men into solitude, simply and solely to serve Thee, and not in any way to gain credit for myself. If I meet my death in trying to put this into execution, Thy Will be done." Without doubt it was a hard thing for him, as it is for everybody, to take the first step, but having once taken it, he began to experience heavenly consolations, and to receive great favours from God. These strengthened him and gave him courage to walk perseveringly in the narrow path of perfection. Having once put his hand to the plough, he never looked back again to what he had left behind, lest he should be found unfit for the kingdom of heaven. The chief defence which he employed against the temptations of the devil, were those two ordinary weapons—prayer and mortification—so earnestly recommended to every Christian. By the first he gained God's powerful assistance, and by the second he succeeded in keeping the domestic enemy chained up, and comparatively powerless. His food at this time consisted of a little parched Indian corn, and even that he partook of but once a day. This custom he maintained throughout the rest of his life, scarcely ever breaking through it, even when prostrated by grievous sickness. As for flesh meat, he entirely forbade himself the use of it. If at times the Indians brought him some as a token of their affection, he accepted it in order not to offend them, and to hide his abstinence, but he never made use of it, at least during this period of his life. Occasionally his solitude was rudely interrupted by a visit from a troop of Spanish soldiers, sent out to scour the country and punish the Indians for their incursions into the settlements. They were always considerably astonished to discover in him a countryman, living in such close proximity to savages, who deemed it a sort of patriotic duty to slay every Spaniard, as being of the hated race which had conquered their land. Their astonishment often gave place to very different sentiments. Some looked upon him as a heretic, who preferred to venture his life among the savages of the forest rather than abjure his errors. Their chief reason for this supposition was, that being in the wilderness, he could not hear Mass. This was a false assumption; for though the nearest station where the Holy Sacrifice was offered was twenty-four miles distant, Gregory nevertheless walked there on all the great festivals to assist at the offices of the Church, and partake of the Holy Communion. Others regarded him as a fool, and took no pains to conceal their opinion from him. They considered his dwelling in such close proximity to the Indians, equivalent to baring his breast to their murderous knives, and would tell him with a grim sort of pleasantry, that he smelt of the grave. In spite of all these forebodings of evil, Gregory lived on, unmolested by the natives, who, though leaving him in peace, ruthlessly murdered every Spaniard who was so foolhardy as to quit the security of the large settlements, and venture into their territory. Not only did he live unharmed among them, but deeply reverenced, we might almost say worshipped. They always approached his little hut with signs of the most profound respect, smiling, bowing, and making salutations to him with their hands. The few necessaries which he required for his daily sustenance were supplied by them, and they deemed themselves highly favoured if they could do him the slightest service. Some few among them who had mixed with the Spaniards, and learnt something of our holy religion, used to enter his abode with the words "Deo Gratias." In fine they were as civil to him, and treated him with as much courtesy and veneration as if he had been one of their kings. Whence did he acquire this ascendency over them? We can only answer, from the indwelling of God's grace in his heart. Its heavenly beauty, and its sweet attractiveness, made themselves manifest in his exterior, and drew these untutored sons of the forest towards him. They perceived that in leaving his own country, he had come to seek treasures of a far different nature, from the vile dross which had led his countrymen from their own land to conquer theirs with fire and sword. In him they saw a man who came, not to rob and to enslave, but to teach them how to trample on the treasures of earth, to serve the Great Spirit as He would have Himself served, and so ensure for themselves admission to the glories of that future existence, about which they had some vague and misty notions.

Not very far from the place where Gregory had built his hermitage, there dwelt a Spaniard named Martin Mrœna. This man, while out hunting or exploring, came one day upon Gregory, who was digging a ditch to fence the little garden, in which he hoped to be able to cultivate a few vegetables for his daily use. Mrœna was astonished beyond all measure, and filled with deep reverential awe, because, as he afterwards testified, he beheld Gregory surrounded by a great company of Angels who guarded him while he worked. This vision filled his soul with such unutterable sweetness, that on his return home, he could not repress the tears of joy that streamed from his eyes. His wife, Doña Maria de Mercada, seeing this, and marking the wonderful change that had come over her husband, earnestly asked of him the cause. After many entreaties he at length yielded to her importunity, and related the vision which God had vouchsafed to him. From this we may form some estimate of Gregory's sanctity, and need not wonder that one thus guarded by the spirits of God, should be secure from all harm amid the bitterest enemies of his race.

CHAPTER III.

HIS TEMPTATIONS AND THEIR REMEDIES.

NO amount of corporal austerities can thoroughly subdue, or effectually crush the domestic enemy which every man carries about with him in his own heart. They may break its strength, or tame its impetuosity, or simply hold it in check, but nothing more. There it is, a living power, abiding within, full of vitality, full of energy, only watching for an opportunity to break loose and assert itself. Such did Gregory find it; such also is the experience of all who would live "a godly life, in Christ Jesus."

They must be content to endure this internal persecution, and to go through the smoke, and dust, and fatigue of the battle field, before they can kneel at the feet of the great Leader to receive upon their brows the crown of victory. Though Gregory had rigorously shut out from his senses everything that could give them any pleasure; though he had denied his eyes the sight of nature's works, and shut his ears to every pleasant sound, and to the rational converse of his fellows; though he had refused to gratify his taste and treated his flesh as one would treat an obstinate beast of burthen; yet he felt, and felt keenly, in his members "the sting of the flesh," and had to wrestle and combat with "the Angel of Satan that was sent to buffet him." In after times, when it was pleasant to think of dangers past, and of battles won, he used to say that he wondered how he had been able to persevere. He declared that now and then, when his imagination brought vividly before him the recollection of those conflicts, his flesh would creep, and his hair stand on end as he remembered the horror with which they used to fill his soul.

One of his greatest friends, who had his entire confidence, relates that during an interview with the holy man, something which occurred in the course of conversation, led Gregory to speak of one of these conflicts.

To use his own homely and graphic language, he said

"that he had had a very hot skirmish with the devil;" and so forcibly did the enemy grapple with him, and so sharp was the struggle requisite to shake him off, that the blood burst out from his ears and nostrils and streamed down upon his neck and breast. How ought those to blush with shame who so easily yield on the slightest assault of the enemy! They say it is hard to resist; that the devil seems to seize upon and hold possession of all their members, and of all their faculties, and that they must of necessity fall. This is not true. No one need fall, or if he does, it is because he wills it. No temptation, or storm of temptation which the devil can raise in our souls, is so powerful as to overwhelm us in spite of ourselves. For God is faithful to us, and will not allow us to be tried beyond our strength. He accommodates the trial to our weakness, in order that we may be able to bear it, and come forth from the conflict triumphant and glorious.

The remedy against all such evils, the weapon which immediately puts us upon an equal footing with our enemies, or rather makes us superior to them, is the remedy, and the weapon of prayer. It was this that Gregory invariably made use of in all his conflicts, and by it he won his battles, and merited his eternal reward. He persevered in it day and night, and with all his might besought God to give him power to subdue his enemy. The form of prayer which he used was very short, but at the same time very efficacious. It consisted of these simple words of the Lord's prayer:—
" Thy Will be done on earth as it is in heaven. Amen.

Jesus." He repeated this continually, if not with his lips, at least with his mind. For the space of three years he never once failed to make this prayer with every breath he drew. Whether he ate, or drank, or worked, or rested, these words ever rose to his lips, or ascended like the sweet odour of incense from his heart, when his lips could not form them into articulate speech. As soon as he awoke from sleep, his first thought embodied itself in the words:—"Thy Will be done," and from that moment till sleep again stole away his consciousness, they arose continually before the throne of God, from the glowing heart of His loving servant. After thus repeating them for the space of three years, and dwelling upon, and as it were drawing all the hidden sweetness and divine efficacy from these inspired words, Gregory, by the impulse of the Holy Spirit, advanced to another exercise. This time it was not one of words or affections to which God moved him, but of works done out of charity for his neighbour. He was filled with a most burning love of God, and this, as was natural, manifested itself in a corresponding love for his neighbour. These two loves are so intimately connected, that the love of God generates (if we may use the expression), the love of our neighbour, and the love of our neighbour nourishes, and keeps the love of God burning brightly in our souls. Built upon so solid a foundation, Gregory went on ascending from virtue to virtue without ever growing lukewarm in charity, and thus reached that state of perfection which Christ wishes all those to attain, who, leaving all things, have followed Him.

CHAPTER IV.

GREGORY LEAVES HIS SOLITUDE, AND GOES TO MEXICO.

THE solitude of the Valley of Amayac began to be very dear and pleasing to Gregory. He loved it, not for its natural beauties, but for the many opportunities it afforded him of sometimes feeling the want, even of those few necessaries which he required for his subsistence. Yet, strong as was his affection for this place which furnished him with so many occasions of mortification, he nevertheless cheerfully abandoned it, because the love he bore his neighbour was stronger still. It must not, however, be supposed that his charity was of that kind which urges men to go out among their fellows and succour them, either in their spiritual necessities, as priests do, in the work of the ministry, or by relieving their temporal wants, like many of the active religious orders. The voice of God within his breast had told him too clearly that such was not his calling. The desert was to be his abode, and there he was to aid his neighbour by his holy life and ceaseless prayer. Yet, when his life there became a scandal to the weak, he did not hesitate for a moment to leave it, because the true solitary can make for himself a desert, even amid the busy haunts of men, and is content to endure the noise and bustle of a great city, either when solitude becomes impossible, or when the utility of others makes it advisable for him to abandon it. It was this latter cause which drew Gregory from the quiet of this secluded valley. Certain rude and ignorant people, seeing that he did not hear Mass on Sundays and festivals, began first to wonder, and then to be scandalized that one who had no possessions, no plantation to care for, should be living where it was impossible for him to attend the public services of the Church. They could not, of course, be supposed to understand how God can call certain devout souls to this kind of life, and that such a call when once sufficiently made evident, exempts those who receive it from the observance of the commandments of the Church, with regard to public worship. This is the opinion of the greatest Theologians, and the practice of devout and learned men in all ages, as we may gather from the fact that in obedience to this call of God's Holy Spirit, the deserts of Egypt and Nitria were peopled with solitaries, some of whom could not, except on the rarest occasions, be present at the holy sacrifice of the Mass.

Gregory knew this very well, and though perfectly convinced that he was justified in pursuing the course he had begun, without paying any attention to what people might say or think of him, he nevertheless did not choose to do so, but, yielding to their weakness and ignorance, removed from his little hermitage, and went to the plantation of a certain Alonzo de Avalos, where it appears he could have the advantage of hearing Mass.

This man received him with the most profound respect

and joy. He was delighted beyond measure at the thought of harbouring one of God's servants, for the very presence of Gregory spoke of communion with the unseen world, and diffused around an odour of sanctity which captivated all beholders, and led them to compunction for their sins, and a desire to serve and love God.

He put his house at Gregory's disposal, and devoted to his sole use, a large garden, beautifully situated, and filled with all those fruits and herbs of which he might stand in need. Perceiving that his guest never ate any flesh-meat, he ordered his steward to appoint an Indian to catch fish for him, that he might at least have something better than bread and water for his nourishment. Gregory gladly accepted the use of the garden, but was very much troubled that any one should be set to work for him, and begged earnestly that no one should be in the slightest degree incommoded by his presence in the house. He would not be satisfied till he had obtained an assurance to this effect from his kind-hearted host, who yielded to his importunity, and let him do as he pleased.

The next two years of his life were spent in this abode of peace. During the whole of that time, he subsisted upon a little milk and curds, of which he partook once every day. When this period had elapsed, the Spirit of God again prompted him to return to his former manner of life, and he at once obeyed. To the unspeakable regret of his worthy host, he made known to him his determination to depart. The following day, therefore, was fixed for his return. After a few hours' rest he arose and sat in his chamber, awaiting the dawn, that he might set out upon his journey at the first glimpse of day. Suddenly the whole earth shook beneath him, the house rocked to and fro, a low rumbling sound, as of subterranean thunder, struck upon his ear, and the very beams of the roof over his head cracked and fell at his feet, but without doing him any harm. This was caused by that terrible earthquake which occurred in the year 1566, and covered the face of Mexico with ruin and desolation. In spite of this dreadful calamity, Gregory went forth, like the just man of the old heathen poet, " fixed in his resolution, and undaunted, though the fragments of the dissolving world came crashing down around him."

As he journeyed onward, he came to the farm of Sebastian Mexia, who entertained him with so much Christian charity, that in order to recompense him for his goodness, he stayed with him for a few days. Mexia was so deeply impressed by his edifying behaviour, and by the words of wisdom, which, sweet as honey, flowed from his mouth, that he determined to put both his estate and himself entirely at the disposal of the holy man, to be directed by him with some of that supernatural wisdom wherewith it was evident that God had endowed him. Suspecting the design of his good host, and knowing, as it would seem, by a species of inspiration, that Mexia's days were numbered, Gregory hastened to quit his hospitable roof, lest after having left all things to follow Christ, he should find himself burthened with the temporal concerns of other men. Bidding adieu, therefore, to Mexia, he once more resumed his journey towards Zacatecas.

At the very time when Gregory returned to his beloved solitude, it happened that Father Dominic de Salazar, a famous Dominican preacher, was engaged in giving missions to the mining population of the district. As far as we have been able to learn, it would seem that they bore a strong resemblance to those who are engaged in a somewhat similar occupation among ourselves. The greed of gold had apparently blotted out of their minds any higher or nobler aspiration than to eat, drink, and be merry, and then, like the beasts that have no understanding, to fall down upon the earth and die. But there had now come among them a man full of the Spirit of God, and eaten up with a burning zeal for His glory, and yet, withal, having a heart for poor sinners, tender as the heart of a mother. His persuasive eloquence softened the hardest hearts, and brought the most obdurate sinners to their knees, humbly craving pardon from God for their many and grievous transgressions. From the people with whom he came in contact, he heard a great deal about Gregory and the wonderful life he was leading, and, as was natural, conceived a great desire to see and be edified by so holy a man. On the first occasion, therefore, that he found himself in the neighbourhood of the hermitage, he went to visit him. He was deeply impressed by his interview with Gregory, and urged him with great earnestness to go to Mexico, to a convent of the Order, where he assured him that he would procure for him a cell and maintenance for the rest of his days. "By this means," said he, "you will be able to persevere in your life of prayer, without any anxiety, and at the same time partake of all the advantages which those only can enjoy who have the happiness of living in community." The counsel of a man so learned, so holy, and so wise, determined Gregory to take the step suggested, and follow the path pointed out to him. He accordingly closed up his little hermitage, and set out for the city of Mexico, after having spent seven years, with the exception of two months, in and about the Valley of Amayac. These two months were seemingly passed in service, for the purpose of gaining a little money to procure clothes. The suit which he had brought with him was now completely worn out, and he was consequently obliged to seek somewhere for another to replace it. With this object in view, he had quitted his solitude, and presenting himself before one of the settlers, had asked for employment. The good man received him with joy, and appointed him as a kind of steward over his estate, to watch over his household, and direct his men in their various offices. This task was accomplished by Gregory with so much sweetness and humility, that he drew the hearts of all to himself. They were filled with admiration for his rare gifts and wonderful sanctity. His simplest words possessed such a charm for them, that their hearts went out to him, and "their very souls knit to his soul." Indeed they would have been happy, could they have kept him with them for this could not be. He must hasten back to the desert which was the dwelling-place appointed for him by God, and there only would the Divine Master speak to his heart. When, therefore, at the end of two months he had gained sufficient money to procure a new outfit, he departed from them. No tears, no entreaties, no offers of food, or raiment, or money could detain him. He left them all in sorrow, but at the same time he left them enriched with his blessing, which produced abundant fruit in due season, as was manifest by the holy lives which all those ever afterwards led, who had had the happiness of being under the same roof with him for those few brief days.

Many persons imagine that such men as Gregory, who have retired from the haunts of men into solitude, never feel any temptation to abandon the life they have undertaken to lead. This is very far from being the case; for, to live after this manner is contrary to flesh and blood, and entails upon those who embrace it, many a long and bitter struggle. It was so with this holy man. As he watched at night in his little hut, the howling of the wild beasts which prowled about in search of food, used at times to fill him with unutterable terror. Then the fearful acts of cruelty practised by the Indians upon the outlying colonists, and their dark deeds of vengeance and of bloodshed, oftentimes presented themselves before him as causes amply sufficient to justify him in leaving that part of the country. Added to all this, there were those fierce interior conflicts with the devil, of which mention has already been made. His life was consequently at times very burthensome to him. He was pressed and straitened on every side above measure, so that he was ready to faint for very weariness, and to cry aloud with the Apostle: "Unhappy man that I am! Who shall deliver me from the body of this death?" Yet for all that, being firmly fixed in the love of God, and full of faith in His sustaining power and fatherly providence, he resisted and persevered, still hoping on against all hope when everything around seemed covered with the dark pall of despair. He persevered, and he conquered. He waited patiently for the Lord, and He gave him the desire of his heart.

In the midst of his temptations there uprose before the throne of God that cry of his heart: "Thy Will be done," and then prostrating himself upon the earth he would say: "Lord, Thou art my Father; everything is done in Thy presence and with Thy Will." After such prayers as these, he arose strengthened and full of comfort, and ready as a giant to run his way. That way was in very deed rough and painful. It was a way of the most abject poverty, and the sharpest self-denial. Yet he never asked an alms from any man. What was offered, he gladly accepted. When every other resource failed, he went forth and worked for the crust of bread that he ate. In consequence of this rigorous method of life, his stomach became very weak, and was a source of great mortification to him for the rest of his days. Occasionally he gave himself a little exercise in a small garden in which he cultivated a few herbs.

But these were very rarely employed for his own use.

Those who passed that way were freely regaled with them, and Gregory rejoiced that he was thus enabled out of his poverty sometimes to help those who were as poor as himself.

CHAPTER V.

HIS RETURN TO THE SOLITARY LIFE.

IN pursuance of the advice given him by Father Dominic, Gregory went to the city of Mexico and presented himself before the Superior of the Dominican Convent. He told him of the counsel which the aforesaid Father had given him, and also of his promise to procure for him a cell and maintenance there for the rest of his days. It would seem that Father Dominic had neglected to make known to the Superior anything of the arrangement he had made, so that the first account of it came from Gregory's own lips, and no doubt caused him considerable astonishment. Father Dominic must, or at least, ought to have known, that permission to dwell in the convent, without becoming a conventual, without, in other words, taking the habit, could not be given. It may possibly have been a pious stratagem on his part for bringing about so happy a consummation. He doubtless thought that Gregory, seeing the devout and regular lives of the Friars, would ultimately be induced to enrol himself among their numbers, and in his eagerness to effect this, forgot that his influence could not procure for the holy man what in his affection and zeal for his Order, he had promised. The Fathers, however, offered Gregory the hospitality of their Convent, and this he thankfully accepted, and remained there some days, hoping that Father Dominic would arrive in the interval and perhaps succeed in making good his word. He probably intimated as much to his kind hosts, but they told him that his hope was vain, for such a thing as Father Dominic had promised was beyond his or their power to grant. Seeing that what he desired could not be obtained, and also feeling that he was not called to a life in community, but to a life of solitude, the holy man presented himself before the Fathers to bid them farewell, and return to the mode of life he had hitherto pursued. Great was the grief of the Friars at being thus obliged to part so soon from him. During the few days he had remained among them, they had seen enough to convince them that his example and his sanctity would have contributed much to their advancement in perfection, and they felt that in losing him, they were losing a treasure of priceless value. But knowing that the gifts of God are various, and that He distributes them broadcast among His children, and does not lead them to His kingdom all by the same way, they consoled themselves with the thought that though Gregory might walk in a way different from their own, the Will of their common Lord was nevertheless being fulfilled.

After he had explained to them his determination to return to the solitary life, they told him of a place which would be admirably suited for him. It was situated far from the settlements, and abounded in a profusion of wild fruits, and of various kinds of herbs which would suffice for his sustenance. The name of this place was Guasteca. Thither Gregory directed his steps, and though he had great reason to fear that it would be very injurious to him, because of the great weakness of his stomach, still, putting a childlike trust in God, he entered upon the life he would have to lead there, in the simple faith that He Who had given the call would likewise supply the strength necessary for him to comply with it. He was in reality glad to leave the Dominican Convent, for he had a secret feeling that he might possibly be a burthen to the Fathers, and this was a thing of which he had a great horror. He was consequently most careful and anxious wherever he went, never in any way to be a source of inconvenience to those with whom he might chance to be.

In his new solitude he continued to lead the same kind of life as he had led in the Valley of Amayac. He lived upon fruit and herbs; he fought valiantly against the temptations and suggestions of the devil, and persevered in the same exercise of the love of God and of his neighbour, whereby he had already made such rapid progress in the way of perfection.

CHAPTER VI.

HIS TRIALS.

IN the solitude of this wild luxuriant country, where nature had scattered abroad with a profuse hand all that suffices for the wants of man, Gregory would have been content to abide for the rest of his days. There, he enjoyed the sweetest contemplation, uninterrupted by the company of men, undisturbed by temporal cares or anxiety for the future. If God had willed it, he would have clung to this beloved solitude till death had closed his eyes to this world, and thrown open for him the portals of his Father's kingdom. But it was not God's Will that this bright and burning light should be hidden under a bushel. It pleased Him that some few, at least, should be consoled and edified by his example, and therefore, He showed him that it was not His Will he should stay there, by withdrawing from him the strength requisite for a life of that nature. He afflicted him with a grievous issue of blood, which His servant bore with exemplary patience for many days. We can easily imagine to what misery and inconvenience he was subjected, if we reflect how utterly destitute he was of all the means and appliances which would have alleviated the pain of his disorder. He was stretched upon a few sheep skins in a miserable hut, with not a single article of household furniture, with not so much as a cup to hold a little water. In this wretched condition he would have been content to drag his emaciated body about from place to place, to obtain the little sustenance he required, till God should be pleased to dissolve his tabernacle of clay, and release his pure soul from its prison-house. But our loving Father has a care of His children even in things temporal, and He so directed matters, that a wayfarer discovered Gregory in his misery, and carried the news of his sad condition to those who were only too happy to relieve it. It was told by some one to Father John de Mesa, a holy and zealous priest, who devoted himself to the service of the poor in those parts, that there was a holy servant of God lying at Guasteca in a very sad plight, and in great need of his charitable offices. Few words were needed to open wide the heart of this Apostle of charity. He sought out Gregory, and having found him, applied such remedies as speedily brought great comfort and relief to God's suffering servant. He had him conveyed to his own house, and there nursed him with all the tenderness of a loving mother. The weakness consequent upon this malady brought Gregory very low,—almost to the verge of the tomb. He was unable to eat anything for many days, and might be said to have had just sufficient vitality left in him to enable him to breathe. At length he fell into a profound sleep, and after reposing for many hours, suddenly awoke, feeling a desire for food. This was given him with a judicious hand, and in a very short time he was perfectly well again. With his returning strength came the desire to go back again to his solitude; but, with a holy importunity this good priest prevailed upon him to remain in his house, and make a solitude for himself there. Gregory at last yielded to his repeated solicitations, and for the space of four years continued to dwell with him. His stay was advantageous to the priest himself, who having so great an example of sanctity continually before his eyes, was urged thereby to press onward in the path of holiness. It tended also very materially to the spiritual profit of the people who dwelt round about. For the fame of his devout life was speedily noised abroad, and attracted to him many who needed direction, or were troubled with doubts, or heavily burthened with the world's cares; and numbers gladly availed themselves of his presence among them to seek relief in their various necessities. Yet though many visited, conversed with, and consulted him, he never divulged his name, nor told his vocation, nor mentioned the exercises he made use of in his continual prayer. In spite, however, of his unmistakable sanctity, there were not a few who looked upon him and the life he led with anything but a friendly eye. These were men of a practical turn of mind, who could see no good or profit in anything that had not some tangible result. They were matter of fact sort of people, hard of head, and given to statistics. Their great objection to Gregory was that he did nothing, but was a sort of vagrant who lived upon the people. If he had taught the children their letters, or their catechism; if he had visited the sick or even kept the small mission chapel clean, it would be something;—but no, he did absolutely nothing! What good therefore was he upon the earth? He was like an unfruitful tree, which was only an incumbrance to the ground. Others went further and whispered abroad that he was a heretic. This was a piece of wanton malevolence, because here at least his position was different from what it had been in Amayac. He had the advantage of living with a priest, of assisting at all the divine offices, and of complying with all the obligations of a good practical Catholic. This accusation then could be the result of nothing else than pure malice. It went so far, that a priest was appointed to examine him, and see if there was any foundation for these reports. After sifting the matter thoroughly, he discovered that the accusation of heresy rested upon nothing weightier than the fact that Gregory did not use beads when saying his prayers, and made no outward sign whatever to indicate the devotion that was within him. Treating these paltry trifles with the contempt which they deserved, the priest determined nevertheless to pay Gregory a personal visit, and see what sort of a man he was, and from his conversation and manners gather some notion of his character. The impression made upon him by this interview was very favourable to Gregory. He found him to be a man of very acute mind, learned in the doctrine of the Church, and seemingly knowing the whole Bible by heart. He looked upon his solitary life as blameless. "He passes most of his time," said he, "in the Church, and treats the world and its affairs as if he were one who had never lived in it. No amount of ingenuity can extort from him any clue by which one might learn something of his parentage. On this subject he is as silent as the grave." Such was the account which he gave to Father Losa, who at that time did not even know Gregory's name. This Father was somewhat amused at the novel reason assigned for considering his future friend a heretic, and said :—" If you saw a thief without his beads, you would not argue therefrom that he was a heretic! Why then should a man so virtuous and so blameless be accounted unsound of faith because he does not use them? The priest replied that he regarded the whole accusation as an absurdity, and that he entertained the highest veneration for Gregory's sublime sanctity. Father Losa then very quaintly remarks, that his informant wound up by saying—"I think I shall present him with a hat, for he wears none." The hat was an article of clothing which Gregory, skilful as he was in other respects, could never succeed in making. There was some mystery also in the construction of shoes which he could never master. When he required these articles, he used, as we have already remarked, to procure some employment in which he could earn a sufficient sum wherewith to purchase them. This casual conversation between the priest and Father Losa, was the occasion which led the latter to cultivate that holy friendship with Gregory, from which he derived so many signal graces and mercies in after years.

CHAPTER VII.

GREGORY RETIRES TO ATRISCO, AND TO THE SANCTUARY OF OUR LADY OF REMEDIES.

NOTHING is more feared by a truly religious and devout man than the spirit of pride. It is so insidious and serpent-like in its approach, it creeps on so stealthily, so noiselessly and imperceptibly, that nothing but the most unremitting vigilance can prevent it from surprising us, and effecting an entrance into our souls. Hence it is that we find the Saints of God seemingly so sensitive, we might almost say morbidly sensitive, and scrupulous on this point. They see danger where we ordinary men see none, and flee from it with an undisguised fear, which, to many, seems unfounded and ridiculous. But they are in the right; for many a one who has crushed the power of sensuality, and trodden it under his feet for a number of years, has at length been shamefully overcome by pride. Why is this? It is because he has not been vigilant. He beheld his greatest enemy, as he thought, under his feet wounded, subdued, and in chains. Deeming everything secure, he slumbered and slept. Then pride stole softly and swiftly in upon him. It entered into his heart unperceived, and took up its abode there. It bound up the wounds of sensuality, its friend and ally. It struck off one by one the links of the chain that held it prisoner. It fanned into a flame the almost extinguished spark of life that still remained in it, and did all this so gradually, that the unwary man had not even a suspicion of its presence within him. Then at length, when all things were ready, his slumber was rudely broken, and he awoke to find himself in the grip of his malignant enemy, to feel that he was bound hand and foot, and hurried from one abyss of infamy to another, even to the very verge of the bottomless pit. Knowing this, we need not be astonished that Gregory should frequently change the place of his abode. He did so, because he feared lest, being puffed up with pride, he should fall away from God; and after guiding others to the very gates of heaven, be himself ignominiously thrust away, and never allowed to enter in through those bright portals. During his stay at Guasteca, the eyes of all had been riveted upon him. All classes of society, Indians as well as Spaniards, testified for him the most unbounded reverence. His words were received almost with the same respect as the inspired words of the Gospel. His advice was followed as exactly as if he had been an angelic messenger, and men actually bowed to him as to a Saint. This was too much for Gregory. He could not endure it. The homage paid to his virtue did not elate him. It rather filled him with fear. He remembered those words of solemn warning: "Let him that thinketh himself to stand, take heed lest he fall," and to make assurance doubly sure that no such thing should ever happen to him, he resolved, like the Fathers of the desert, to flee away from the intercourse of men. His determination was no sooner taken than he at once put it into execution. He left the house of De Mesa, and turned his face towards the district lying round the town of Atrisco. As he journeyed onward and had come within three miles of the city, he met a man of great wealth and consideration in those parts, named John Perez Romero. They accosted each other and fell into conversation, the upshot of which was, that Romero prevailed upon Gregory to go with him, and to consider his house henceforth as his future home. Gregory found his new abode everything that he could desire. The family of Romero was what a good Christian family ought to be. They were devout, full of faith and of the fear of God, and zealous in all works of charity. Apter scholars to learn the science of salvation could not be found, and they were not slow to discover what manner of man their guest was, but eagerly profited by his presence among them to follow his good counsel, and practise the lessons he taught. Gregory therefore applied himself diligently to feed this little flock which he had found in the wilderness, repaying them thus by spiritual blessings for their charitable ministration to his temporal wants. Silver and gold he had none, but what he had he gave them, and that was detachment from the things of earth, and a more determined pursuit of that one thing necessary,—the salvation of their immortal souls. He found the country round about very beautiful. The air, though mild and balmy, was not relaxing. On all sides he beheld fruitful fields, watered by streams, pure and clear as crystal. The vegetation was varied and luxurious. The woods teemed with game, the rivers were full of fish. In a word, God seemed to have poured forth His choicest blessings upon this lovely spot, with a profuse bounty which could not fail to draw from the most thoughtless observer a hymn of thanksgiving and of praise. All this agreed very well with Gregory, and gave him fresh vigour to serve the Lord with redoubled fervour. It was not, however, the Will of the great Master that he should remain in this quarter very long. He had scarcely been there two years when the devil began to stir up some of the more ignorant of the people against him. But the malignity of this wicked spirit served only to work out the designs of God, Who alone can bring forth good out of evil; for Gregory was led by reason of the storm raised against him, and the consequences that flowed from it, to become a source of edification unto many more than would otherwise have had the advantage of his holy example. As in the days of the Apostles, it was the pious and good who at the instigation of certain evilly-disposed persons, raised the persecution whereby Paul and Barnabas were cast out of Antioch, so also did it happen in the case of Gregory. Many who had more piety than knowledge, and more zeal than discretion, took offence at the life he was leading. Seeing in one so young such gravity of manner, united with so much wisdom and science, and that too without his ever having studied at any University, they began to fear that something was not right. Possibly he might have come by all this wisdom through very questionable means,—likely enough through the agency of the devil. If that were the case, he was doubtlessly living thus secretly and under the cloak of great austerity with some sinister design upon the population at large. And thus, one pious soul added to the fears of another, till such a story was spread abroad about Gregory, who was totally unconscious of the excitement he was creating, that it was thought advisable to lay it before the Archbishop of Mexico.

Whatever the original version of that story may have been, no one can tell; but by the time it had reached the ears of the ecclesiastical authorities, it had assumed a form so strange and monstrous, that they thought it necessary to institute a commission to inquire into and search the matter to the very bottom. An examination was accordingly made into the whole of Gregory's life, the result of which was, that the Archbishop himself, by a public and solemn act, bore witness to the extraordinary piety, virtue, and innocence of the holy man.

This was more than Gregory's humility could endure. Had he been censured by the commission, he would have rejoiced in having something to suffer; but since the members who composed it had openly expressed their admiration of him, and their approval of all that he had done, he thought it high time to depart from a locality where there were so many snares set to rob him of his virtue. He, therefore, went straightway to Romero, and asked his leave to depart. The good man tried in vain to detain him. His family added their tears to his earnest entreaties. But though the heart of Gregory was moved, for he loved them all dearly, he still persisted in his determination to go, and turned a deaf ear to all their prayers. Then, with tearful eye and faltering voice, he invoked a blessing upon them, and they saw his face no more.

Once again he was a homeless wanderer upon the face of the earth. But though homeless, he was not friendless. The guiding hand of his Divine Master still held and directed him to a place where there was work for him to do. Under the leading of that loving Father, he journeyed on hopefully, with his face towards the city of Mexico. When he had arrived at a little place called Tescuco, which was but a few miles from the city, he lifted up his eyes and looked about him. Before him lay the city itself, which even in his day presented an imposing appearance to the spectator, as it lay in the centre of an elevated plain, almost surrounded by lofty hills. On one of these bold eminences there had been built, in a most splendid situation, a house and sanctuary dedicated to our Lady of Remedies. This noble structure at once attracted his attention, and a conviction immediately took possession of him, that this was the goal towards which the hand of God had been guiding him. He therefore made directly for it, and without passing through Mexico arrived at the sanctuary, full of hope that he might find there the means of leading a solitary and devout life. Great was his joy when he learnt that this institution was dedicated to the most holy Mother of God. This was one reason the more to induce him to take up his abode there, and live as one of her most humble and devoted servants. Accordingly, after some time spent in earnest prayer, he determined to stay there, and then waited calmly for God to bring about the accomplishment of this purpose. For some months nobody took any notice of him further than to remark that he seemed very devout, and had the appearance of a simple man, of little ability and weak understanding. During that time his sufferings from want of food must have been very great; for since he never asked for alms, but always waited till the hearts of the charitable were moved to bestow them upon him, his condition was worse than that of the most abject mendicant. Nevertheless, he abided patiently for the moment when God should deem it fitting to send him succour, and in the mean time appeased the cravings of hunger by eating the wild quinces that grew in the hedges by the way-side. His trust in God was not in vain, for after a time the pious faithful who visited the sanctuary began to notice him, and to admire the evident holiness of his life. First one, and then another, invited him to dine with them, and thus his method of life became known to them, and raised in their minds a high esteem for him. It was most probably in the houses of these good Samaritans that he found shelter for some part of the time, though it is certain that he must have lived also at the hospice itself. Father Losa is not at all clear about the means by which he gained admittance into it, or whether he gained admittance at all. We must, then, take it for granted that he had a lodging there, since his biographer seems to insinuate as much in his narrative. Though the greater number of those who came in contact with Gregory during his stay at the sanctuary were edified by his conversation and bearing, still there were some who did not by any means approve of his life, as it was altogether out of the common. Not a few looked upon him as little better than an impostor and idle vagabond. Others went so far as to say that he was a concealed heretic, and would have nothing whatever to do with him. His sufferings from these people were very great. What the specific nature of them was, we have not been able to learn. Gregory himself never mentioned them, for he always bore "the slings and arrows of outrageous fortune," with the profoundest silence and resignation. No eye witnessed his pain but the eye of Him " Who seeth and judgeth," and knoweth how to reward both the persecutor and the persecuted according to their works. As the evil that is said about men is more rapid in its flight and more easily disseminates itself than the good, the reports that were in circulation about Gregory reached the Archbishop's ears long before any of the edifying traits of his character, or the wonderful gifts and graces with which God had endowed him. Like a watchful shepherd, whose duty it was, in accordance with the customs and laws of that time, to search out heresy and preserve his flock from the contagion of it, he ordered a careful scrutiny to be made into the life and manners of Gregory. At the very time that this order was issued, Father Losa paid him a visit, and from the interview he had with him, conceived a very high estimate of his sanctity.

He told the Archbishop of the impression that had been made upon him by his conversation with Gregory, but the prelate did not alter his determination in the least on that account. He wished to institute a most minute and searching examination into all that had been said about him, that thus he might fully satisfy his own conscience, and set the matter at rest for ever. For this purpose he selected Alonzo Sanchez, a Father of the Society of Jesus. He instructed him to inquire into the employments which occupied his time, the spiritual exercises he made use of, the kind of prayer in which he addressed himself to God, the austerities he practised, and the rest. In one word, Sanchez, morally speaking, had to dissect him, to make a study of him, and then report of what he should see and hear. He accordingly repaired to the Sanctuary of our Lady of Remedies, and for some considerable time made it his business to visit and hold frequent conferences with the holy man, without, however, letting it appear that he had come for that express purpose, and with full authority to put him upon his trial.

To all questions upon his faith, his customs, and his spirit, Gregory answered with so much humility, brevity, and caution, that Sanchez was amazed, and knew not precisely what to make of him. There was raised in his mind a very great desire to know the whole truth about him, and thinking that the best plan to get at this would be openly to announce to him that he had been sent as his judge by the competent authorities, he one day summoned him into his presence, and with great severity addressed him thus:—"We must be free and open with each other. I am here by the authority of the Archbishop, whose duty it is to know all his sheep. I am here to obtain a complete insight into your life and manners. Answer me, therefore, clearly and plainly upon all those points upon which I shall question you."

Gregory, with great meekness and humility, answered: —" It is but fitting that I should obey my pastor and prelate, and your Reverence in his name." After this Sanchez began his scrutiny. He was a man of extensive learning, and well versed in all spiritual matters. From long experience, he had become profoundly skilled in reading and understanding the human heart. He began then to sift Gregory anew. He piled question upon question, and tried to involve him in the subtilties of the schools. He put the most intricate propositions to him on matters of faith and morals. To all of them Gregory gave a clear and precise answer, grounding his reply upon sacred Scripture, and relating the heresy that had arisen upon the subject, with the chief errors contained in it, the life of the heretic who had broached them, and the lives of the chief Doctors who had been raised up by God to maintain the truth. The authorities he cited to prove his statements were so well chosen, so much to the point, and so weighty, and the language he used so elegant and polished, that the Father was completely astounded. His wonder was still further increased when, after hurling objection upon objection against Gregory's answers, the holy man solved them all with the ease of one who had stood the brunt of such intellectual battles for many years in the schools. The vast stores of knowledge, theological and otherwise, displayed by him in this trial, made so deep an impression upon Sanchez, that he was not only completely satisfied with him, but conceived a great respect and love for his person.

He gave a detailed report of these interviews to the Archbishop, who was exceedingly pleased that a man of so much virtue and learning had entered his Diocese and become one of his flock. From that time forward he caused him to be made much of, and frequently honoured him with a personal visit.

The Archbishop one day said to Father Losa, shortly after the examination held by Sanchez: "The good Jesuit, among other encomiums passed upon Gregory, said to me: 'Compared with this man, my Lord, I have not yet learnt my spiritual alphabet.'"

CHAPTER VIII.

GREGORY REMOVES TO THE HOSPITAL OF GUASTECA.

GREGORY remained two years at the House of our Lady of Remedies. He had now been leading this solitary kind of life for seventeen years, and the austerities he had practised in it began to tell upon him, and to cause him great suffering. He was tortured by very severe pains in his stomach, which made the taking of the little sustenance he allowed himself, a species of martyrdom.

The situation also of the place where he dwelt was

very trying to him. It was built high up among the hills, and the keen, strong winds that swept over it were little suited for one so delicate as Gregory. His removal was therefore rendered necessary in order to preserve his life. He was consequently transferred to the Hospital of Guasteca, which is in the Marquisate of Vallé, about thirty-six miles from Mexico.

As soon as the Archbishop heard that this had been determined upon, he sent a horse to carry him, and a servant to attend him on his journey. Father Losa accompanied his friend part of the way. He could not go with him as far as his new abode, because of his parochial duties in the city. This happened in the year 1580, when Gregory was about thirty-eight years old. The esteem in which he was held by all, was testified by the anxiety which every one displayed to possess something that had belonged to him. This was a matter of some difficulty, since his whole earthly property consisted of three sheepskins which served him for a bed, and an earthen pitcher, in which he kept a little fresh water. Father Losa very naïvely informs us, that he had an eye upon one of these sheepskins for himself, but though he was Curate of the Cathedral, he could not obtain it. Others had been before him, and had carried off the precious relic.

In due time, Gregory, attended by the Archbishop's servant, arrived at the Hospital, and was received by Brother Stephen de Herera. At this time the institution was very small, so that only a limited number of patients could be accommodated. That number happened to be filled up when Gregory came, and yet this excellent man received him, and ordered him to be placed in his own apartments, and tended with the utmost care.

In this he simply followed out the desire of their Superior, whose will it was that the same care and consideration should be bestowed upon all who came to them, without any distinction whatsoever. The number of those for whom they provided was very great, and though the house was small, and the revenue insufficient, yet the air was so health-giving, and the blessing of God upon the labours of the Brethren so fruitful, that they never failed amply to supply the wants of the poor, and to effect their speedy restoration to health. Viewed from a merely human and rational stand-point, this may have been attributable in great measure to the salubrity of the position in which the Hospital was built; but much was doubtless owing to the favour with which Almighty God looked down upon that courageous and truly christian man, Bernardine Alvarez, who founded the Asylum for the infirm and poor. Other institutions of a similar character were raised by him in Mexico, and on all of them God's blessing was evidently bestowed. When Father Losa asked him to allow Gregory to be received into his house, he made an answer which shows us the large-heartedness and Christlike love of the sick and poor, which was his characteristic mark. "Would to God," he said, "Reverend Father, that I could bring into my Hospital all the poor in the world! For I have very great confidence in Jesus Christ, that He would keep

4—2

them all. I gladly therefore accede to your request." The event proved that his trust in God was not misplaced. Within two years after its establishment, the house at Guasteca could afford support for seventy-five persons. It went on increasing year by year, till it seemed as if God had "set up a table in the wilderness at which all the poor and needy might eat." They came from all parts of New Spain, Spaniards and Indians, men, women and children, for they found such good treatment provided, so much care taken, and the very air of the place so balmy and healthful, that to be under its roof seemed to be a sufficient guarantee for a complete restoration to health. People attributed many of the blessings bestowed upon this famous Hospital to the fact that Gregory Lopez had been there shortly after its first commencement. His life there was very much the same as it had been in solitude, only that he was now free from all care about his maintenance, though that made very little difference to him, for he never troubled himself about what the morrow might bring forth. He now employed himself wholly in contemplation, and by means of mental exercises, tried to perfect himself daily more and more in the love of God and of his neighbour. The exercises by which he endeavoured to accomplish this were indeed the same, but the improvements he daily introduced into them were different. He had a little chamber or cell for his own particular use, whence he never issued except on Sundays and holidays to hear Mass. If he was unable through some accident to do this in the chapel of the Hospital, he used to go to the Convent of St. Dominic. He now began to deny himself the gratification of looking upon the magnificent scenery which surrounded him. This was exceptionally rich and gorgeous, but it was for him a garden closed up, a sealed book, the eloquence of whose pages he allowed not to speak to his heart. It was not that he was incapable of appreciating such beauties keenly; on the contrary, his was a soul to which nature spoke in her thousand tongues, with a language of such melodious sweetness, as to make every fibre of his heart thrill with ecstatic pleasure. Yet he closed up the avenues of his senses through which her words might find entrance, lest the charms of created things should take away his thoughts and affections from Him, of Whom all earthly beauty is but a faint shadow, and a very imperfect reflection.

Though living in the Hospital, he very rarely visited the sick. The diseases which they laboured under were, generally speaking, of a very nauseous character, and the bad odour arising from the sores and wounds of the poor afflicted patients, easily turned his stomach and caused him great pain. This absence from the scene of suffering was soon noticed by a certain class of people, who seem to be constitutionally censorious, and their remarks upon it were severe and cutting. They could not see why Gregory should confine himself all day to his room, and never render the slightest assistance in the ordinary work of the establishment, when the help of every one in it barely sufficed to meet the demands of the sick. This is an old grievance against those who devote themselves to a life of contemplation. Martha ever complains of Mary; yet a high authority has declared that Mary's is the better part. But though Gregory did not take an active share in the work, those who were enlightened could clearly perceive that the efficacy of his prayers did more for the advancement of the Hospital in its sphere of usefulness, than the united efforts of the busiest and most zealous attendants. He had a special talent for managing those of the patients who were deemed by the Brothers unmanageable. When they were angry, or petulant, or grumpy, no one could bring them to reason sooner than Gregory. When they refused medicine from all other hands, Gregory could prevail upon them to take it from his. When they were low spirited, and allowed their miseries to get the better of them, no one could win back a smile to their dejected faces sooner than he. Hence in this respect his presence in the Hospital was no small advantage and help to its wellbeing; for when asked to do these kind offices he never refused to comply, though Alvarez had by a special privilege exempted him from all obligation of attending to the wants of the patients. Gregory's reputation for sanctity increased more and more every day. It frequently brought to him men renowned for their virtues and learning, who invariably left him full of admiration for the wonders God wrought in his person. Among others who visited him at this time was Father Peter de Pravia, of the Holy Order of St. Dominic. This was a man whose great intellectual power was surpassed only by his unaffected piety and childlike humility. He had first been a Lector of theology in his own Order, and was afterwards advanced to the important post of Vicar-General of the Archdiocese of Mexico. When a Bishopric was offered to him, he refused it, out of a deep sense of his own unworthiness, though he himself was the only person who could not recognise that he had all the qualities requisite for the worthy discharge of so high an office. His visit was made for the express purpose of making a searching inquiry into the life and exercises of Gregory. He was doubtless moved to do this by weighty motives, but he never assigned the reason for this step. What conclusion he arrived at, after a diligent examination of the holy man, is not known; but Father Losa remarked that ever after, he treated Gregory with the utmost deference and respect, as being a man of very extraordinary sanctity.

The Bishop of Guadalaxara also made a very minute inquiry into the life Gregory had led during the seven years he had resided in his Diocese. His testimony of him was to the effect, that though the devil did his utmost to obscure the fame of this servant of God, by raising up against him all sorts of damaging reports, yet, like true metal, he always came forth from the crucible of trial, purer and more resplendent.

During his residence at this Hospital, Gregory employed his time, without detriment to his prayer and contemplation, in the compilation of a book on Medicine for the use of the Brothers who had the care of the sick. In this work he displayed a most extraordinary amount of knowledge concerning the natural properties of herbs, and made prescriptions to be used in compounding medicine, which showed as much learning and skill as if he had been all his life engaged in the practice of the healing art. The Brothers found this work of the greatest use to them, and by following its directions, succeeded in effecting many wonderful cures. Hence, even in a material point of view, Gregory was of great use to the institution which had so charitably received him, and contributed much to its reputation and practical utility.

CHAPTER IX.

SICKNESS COMPELS GREGORY TO GO TO MEXICO, AND THENCE TO SANTA FÉ.

WONDERFUL are the ways which Providence makes use of to cause holy men to be sent from place to place! It happens at times that some of God's favoured souls need the help of a particular individual, and He thereupon manages human affairs in such a way, that the right man is somehow or other put into the right place, though that place may seem, both to himself and to his neighbours, to be of all others the least suitable for him. It was so with Gregory. He had thought over and over again, that the spot where he had taken up his abode was to be his dwelling, till the summons should come, to call him hence to his eternal home. Frequently had he in different places applied to his little cell these words of the Psalmist:—" This is my

rest for ever and ever, here will I dwell because I have chosen it." God, however, in various ways ordained it otherwise, as we have already seen. On this particular occasion it was sickness which drove Gregory from his solitude. His malady was but an instrument in God's hands to conduct him to another place, where " the children, it might be, were calling for bread, and there was no one to break it to them." Accordingly, by the permission of God, he was attacked by the scarlet fever. For several days he strove to resist, and shake it off; but it had already taken a firm hold upon him. His head was on fire, and ached with a heavy, dull, monotonous pain. His throat was parched and sore. At times he was burning with heat, and anon trembling with cold. He yielded at length after three days to its power, and went to bed. The physician who attended him was apparently not a very wise one, but adhered in a wooden sort of way to his rules. One of these, we should be led to suppose, was that famous dictum:—
" *Calida frigidis, et frigida calidis curantur ;*" for in order to rid Gregory of the fiery heat that was in his veins, he bled him, not once or twice, but as often as fourteen times! How the poor man survived such treatment is a marvel, considering his previously weak state of health. He did not die as might naturally have been expected, but was preserved by God's power to labour for His glory, and be useful to many who needed his counsel and instruction. As is usually the case in sickness of this kind, the fever left a malady behind it, as it were in token of its visit. In Gregory's case there

was great heat in his blood, and an inflammation of the liver.

This necessitated his removal to a cooler part of the country, where he might rest a little and recover from the effects of his disorder.

About nine miles from Mexico lies the flourishing little town of St. Augustine. Thither it was thought fit to remove him, and as there dwelt there a certain John de Escobar who, when Gregory was at Guasteca, had invited him to come and dwell with him, he was taken to his house. On arriving there he wrote a letter to Father Losa acquainting him with the happy termination of his little journey. Father Losa was just about to mount his horse and ride out to Guasteca to visit him, when this letter was put into his hand. Turning the horse's head towards St. Augustine, he soon reached Escobar's abode, and was immediately led to the bedside of his friend. He found him poorly lodged and badly attended, and determined at once to have him removed to Mexico. He effected this without delay, and having transported him back to the city, kept him in his own house. Here, as usual, he was visited by many devout people who came to consult him in their doubts and interior trials. The good which he effected in their regard was immense, so that people saw in his coming a merciful favour granted by God for the salvation of many. The only place to which he went during his stay, was the Jesuits' College, where he occasionally heard Mass. The Viceroy's wife earnestly desired to see and converse with him, and often entreated Father Losa to introduce her to him, but all efforts to bring this about were vain. To every appeal Gregory only answered: "I have no need of the Lady Marchioness, nor the Lady Marchioness of me." Years after when he heard that this noble lady and her husband had somehow or other fallen into bad odour with the Government, and were not in such prosperity as formerly, he said: "Now I would visit the Marchioness if she sent for me." Mexico, though it did much towards his recovery, did not work a perfect cure. The fever still hung about him, as if it had never left his veins. He felt greatly prostrated and weak, and had no appetite for the little nourishment which he took once every day. His heart also was not perhaps quite at ease, for he sighed after his beloved solitude. He had endeavoured to observe it as far as possible in the house of his kind host, but after all it was only a fictitious solitude. Though he would not look on the face of nature, yet he longed to be where there were open fields, where he could hear the rippling of the river, and the roar of the mountain torrent. He missed the chatter of the gay birds, and the cries of the wild animals, and the stillness of the summer eventide. Father Losa, perceiving this, went out to search for some place near the city where he might have both the retirement of the country, and yet not be so far removed from the town, as to deprive his friends of the benefit of his holy conversation. In the course of his rambles he went to a little village called Santa Fé, which is situated about six miles from Mexico. He was very pleased with its appearance and the delightful temperature of the air, the verdure of its trees, and the crystal clearness of its streams. He at once fixed upon it as a suitable place for Gregory. The village was under the government of the Dean and Chapter of the church of Mechoacan. Father Losa communicated his desire to Dr. Hernando Ortez, Canon of the Cathedral of Mexico, and Rector of Santa Fé. This good priest, zealous for the promotion of piety in his district, gladly gave his consent to allow Gregory to reside in a little house some short distance from the town, close to the banks of the river. He also gave orders that the Indians should provide him with whatever he needed, and charge it to the hospital which belonged to the church of Mechoacan.

When this permission had been obtained, Gregory entered into solitude on the twenty-second of May, 1589. He never left it again till they carried him forth to his last resting-place in the grave.

CHAPTER X.

GREGORY'S LIFE AND DAILY EXERCISES AT SANTA FÉ.

IN his new abode, Gregory continued to lead what we should call his old life; but to him it was ever new. For the first seven months after going to Santa Fé, he spoke to no one, except, indeed, it were to Father Losa, who visited him occasionally. On Sundays and festivals, he went abroad, to enjoy the privilege of assisting at the Divine Mysteries; and when in presence of his Lord, though silent, he preached most eloquently by his modest deportment, and by the sanctity that shone through him, and riveted the eyes of all beholders.

For some time his great friend and admirer, Father Losa, had felt an inward call, when watching Gregory, which bade him "Go and do in like manner." He was an acute and wary man; one not easily led away by impulse. He quietly searched the spirit, "to see if it were from God," and sat down deliberately to weigh the expense; "to see if he had wherewith to build," and thus save himself the confusion of having the finger of ridicule pointed at him, as a man who had begun a great work and could not finish it. We therefore find him making use of all the means within his reach, to discover if it were the Will of God that he also should become a Solitary. He prayed much himself, and procured others to do the same for him. He also took counsel that he might understand the light in which others might look upon the step; for there were many who did not favour it at all. They argued, that having been Curate of the great Church for more than twenty years, and actively engaged in works of charity, especially in that of relieving the shame-faced poor, it would be rash for him to throw himself into a state of complete inactivity, and thus suddenly reverse the whole current of his life. Besides, they considered the great good he was effecting among the people, and thought that it would be an abandonment of duty to leave his employment and go into solitude. The various sides of the question were laid before his Superiors, and after giving the matter due consideration, they at length consented to allow him to retire from active life, and join his friend in solitude.

Upon obtaining permission, Father Losa made all possible haste to quit his parish, and towards Christmas, in the year 1589, took up his abode in the house where Gregory dwelt. From that day forth, he had the privilege of living with him till he had performed for him the last office of friendship, by closing his eyes in death. Having now many more opportunities of observing the holy man, he resolved to put his high estimation of him to a severe test. He watched him narrowly, and with a severe and critical eye, to discover if familiarity with him might not breed contempt, or lower in him the lofty idea his life had hitherto excited. But the virtue of the servant of God was proof even against this. The more narrowly and critically he examined him, and his method of life, the higher did his love and veneration for him rise. Every day his spirit seemed more admirable, his virtues more heroical, and his life more heavenly.

It was to the observations he made during this residence with Gregory, that we are indebted for the little that we know of the holy man's life. But, unfortunately, never dreaming that he might survive his friend, and never imagining that he would ever have to become his biographer, he did not commit to writing all that he saw or heard. Hence much that might have been very profitable to us has been lost, what we know being but a tithe of what we might have learnt, had he watched him with the ulterior intention of publishing the result of his observations. It is on this plea that Father Losa excuses himself for not recording more minutely the sayings and doings of his friend. However, since one day of his life resembled very much the day that preceded it, and the one that followed it, we may, by observing him through its succeeding hours, have a very correct idea of the manner in which he lived.

He rose at daybreak, and throwing open his casement, drew up the order of what he intended to do during the day. Being scrupulously neat and clean, he next performed the duties of the toilet with great care. Then followed a lecture from the Bible, which lasted for a quarter of an hour. This sacred Book was ever looked upon by him as a letter sent from God; and, though he might not perfectly understand what he read at one time, still the light to do so would be granted to him at another. So great was the respect he had for the Sacred Scripture, and so constant his perusal of it, that his conduct for each day was grounded upon the morning lecture which he daily took from its pages. We may gather from what he said a few days before his death, how perseveringly he had adhered to this practice. "For these last ten days," said he, "I have not read my Bible. I do not remember to have omitted this practice for so long a time, since I began to lead a solitary life."

After closing the sacred Book, he gave himself up to a spiritual exercise, so internal, so secret, so free from any outward sign which might have betrayed its nature, that no one could detect whether it were prayer, or meditation, or contemplation. No one could tell whether he spoke to God, or whether God spoke to him. One could merely conclude, from the modesty and composure of his person, and the sweet gravity of his countenance, that he was in the presence of his God, without for a moment losing sight of Him. What we have already recorded concerning this prayer was told to Father Losa by Gregory, in the course of various conversations held at different times upon the subject, when it happened to be incidentally introduced. He also made some revelations regarding his prayer to Don Dominic de Salazar, who was at this time Bishop of the Philippines. This prelate, when a simple priest, had visited Gregory, as we related in the fourth chapter. He was now on his way from Mexico to Spain, and learning that Gregory was at Santa Fé, came to pay him a visit, out of the love and respect he bore for him. Nothing could exceed his joy at again meeting with one who had inspired him with so much affection and veneration. They conversed long together, and the Bishop, among other questions, asked Gregory what exercise he used when in prayer, and what were the sentiments with which God inspired him. He answered without hesitation: "The exercise I use in my prayer, is the love of God and of my neighbour." "That," replied the Bishop, "is the very answer you gave me in Amayac, five and twenty years ago! How is this? Have you been practising this one thing ever since?" "Yes," replied he, "I have ever done this; though there is a difference between the work done then, and that which is done now."

By this answer we may understand that the exercise of God's holy presence, as practised by him, was practised in no dry and barren way, but was ever accompanied by an intense love of God and of his neighbour. This, as we are told in the Scripture, is the very summit of perfection; at least, of such perfection as is attainable in this world.

In this way, then, did Gregory spend the day, and a great part of the night. These were his prayers, these his meditations, and the food whereon his soul fed and was nourished. In these he employed himself all day, but it was observable that in the morning he was more completely absorbed in them than in the afternoon.

He had no fixed place for his exercises of prayer, nor did he restrict himself in the performance of it to any particular posture. In these merely accidental matters, he was very large minded. Sometimes he knelt in his chamber, at others he would stand or sit, or even walk about in the little corridor which led to his room. In his latter days, when through the great weakness of his body he could not kneel, but was forced to sit or recline, he used to console himself with the thought that God attends more to the disposition of our souls, than to the posture of our bodies, when we lift up our hearts in prayer to Him.

Towards eleven o'clock, Father Losa and Gregory dined together, and also any guest who might happen to be there, for Gregory did not object to any one being with him on these occasions, especially if he were an ecclesiastic or a religious. The conversation was generally on matters of piety, or of things from which something good and useful might be extracted. Gregory had great skill and tact in doing this, and was consequently a very great source of edification to others. For a short time after the meal the same kind of discourse followed, and when any religious person was present, it was wonderful to see how appositely Gregory could speak, though he never began a subject, nor uttered a word unless he were asked some question, or when he saw that the occasion required it.

When no guest happened to be present, or when conversation flagged, Father Losa read a chapter from such works as Villega's "*Flos Sanctorum*," the "Chronicles of St. Francis," the "*Pratum Spirituale*," and the like. When this was ended, Gregory retired to his room, to apply with greater earnestness of soul to that union with God, which external business never entirely interrupted, but only diminished in its intensity. When alone in his chamber, he never allowed sleep to close his eyes or steal away his senses, thus procuring for himself more time to devote to God, and depriving himself of that repose, which in so hot a climate is almost a necessity. In the afternoon he would admit any one who wished to confer with him on matters pertaining to the spiritual life. There was with him no exception of persons; he received the poor peasant as readily as he would the highest functionary in the settlement. To all he gave counsel and comfort, so that they always went away encouraged, and light of heart, with a manly, christian determination to face and conquer their difficulties. It was not for spiritual advice alone that men resorted to Gregory. His wisdom was so great, and his intellect so keen, that in matters of great weight, those high in office used to refer their difficulties to him. Some came to him in person, others wrote letters explaining their case, and asking his counsel. Among the most illustrious of these was Don Louis de Valesco, Marquis of Salinas; he was President of the Council, had been twice Viceroy of New Spain, and once of Peru. He had a wonderful affection and respect for Gregory, and whenever he came to visit him, remained closeted with him for hours. Gregory was to him an able counsellor, not only in matters that regarded his soul, but also in the intricate affairs of his public government. The afternoon was thus spent in receiving visits and in giving advice to those who came to ask for it. Towards sunset he retired to his chamber, which he never left till next morning at sunrise. When the darkness came on, he denied himself the solace of a light. Some used to wonder how he could do anything, thus deprived of light, forgetting that his exercises, being all internal, needed not any material light; the illumination of the Spirit within was sufficient for him. He eat no supper, and remained thus alone in the dark till about half-past nine, when he usually retired to rest. This rest was taken lying on a very mean rug, spread upon the ground. It lasted, as far as Father Losa's observation could compute, for about three hours. The remaining time, till sunrise, was spent in holy contemplation and devout communion with God. Thus were the years passed at Santa Fé, in the same unvarying manner, till God was pleased to call His servant to his eternal rest.

CHAPTER XI.

HIS LAST ILLNESS AND DEATH.

THE hour of Gregory's deliverance "from the body of this death," was fast drawing nigh.

Early in the month of May, 1596, he began to feel a little indisposed, and though the symptoms showed nothing to cause any alarm, still there was a something about them which made the holy man feel as he had never felt before, and convinced him that this time it was the hand of death that had touched him, and was beckoning him away. Slowly but steadily the disease increased. His stomach soon refused all food; it was with difficulty that he could swallow even a little liquid to moisten his throat. To add to his discomfort and pain, the issue of blood, with which he had been troubled once before, returned again. Father Losa, seeing him thus gradually becoming worse and worse, would have sent for a doctor to prescribe for him, but Gregory would not permit him to do so. From his own great knowledge of medicine, and from the practical skill he had acquired in treating the special malady from which he was suffering, he saw perfectly well that a doctor would be of no use to him, and would only increase instead of diminish it. The strong remedies which a physician was sure to apply, would only serve to exhaust the little strength which yet remained in him, without being able to expel the disease. Seeing the anxiety of Father Losa to procure an experienced practitioner, and his diligence in applying remedies, he said to him with a quiet smile: "My good Father, let us walk at God's pace." He tried by these words to teach him that when trouble and misfortune come upon us, it is a time for resignation to God's Will, and not for fretting and chafing in our feeble effort to do what surpasses our strength and our skill. One of his favourite sayings on this subject was, "Resignation is all deeds, it hath no words."

For some days there was no alteration in his condition, either for better or for worse. There was the same dull, monotonous round of pain, which he bore with the same heroic resignation as he had manifested in his other sicknesses. At length, on the twenty-fourth of June, the festival of the great St. John the Baptist, Father Losa thought that his illness had become so dangerous, that it was time to administer to him the Most Holy Sacrament. When he asked him if he were willing to receive the Holy of Holies, with his usual simplicity and absence of all display or affectation, Gregory merely said "Yes," adding, "I am glad that I shall receive the Viaticum on this day, because I have taken St. John for my special advocate and patron."

The good Father accordingly administered to him the most Holy Sacrament, that strength of the weak, that heavenly bread, in the might of which poor feeble mortals enter in through the dark portals of death, and press onward up the mountain of God till they reach His awful presence. They do so with confidence, for they bear in their hearts Jesus Christ, the dearly beloved Son of the Just Judge, before Whom they are about to give an account of all the deeds done in the body.

Father Losa did not give him Extreme Unction, but kept the holy oil close at hand to be in readiness, if any sudden attack should seize upon his friend. His pulse was very low, and the beat was at times almost imperceptible. It will give us some notion of his great determination and courage, to know that on the day he received the Viaticum, and also on those days that followed, in spite of his great weakness, he rose from his bed, dressed himself, and put his little room in order. Till the very day of his death he would never allow any one to assist him in the various necessities incident to a sick man, but went about them all unaided by any one.

Day by day his strength ebbed slowly away. He could not eat, but was kept alive by stimulants, which his friends in Mexico sent to sustain him. Reflecting upon this, as he lay upon his poor couch, he used to say with deep feeling: "Thou art wonderful in Thy ways, O Lord! Here am I, a man not possessing the value of a pin, and yet when I need the drink of the rich and noble to sustain my life, there are persons at hand to bestow it upon me, without my asking."

When the festival of the holy Apostles, SS. Peter and Paul came, Father Losa, thinking he would not outlast the day, told him that he would now give him the sacrament of Extreme Unction. The joy of Gregory was very great, not only for the reception of the sacrament, but because it was to be administered to him on the festival day of the two great princes of the Church. Before proceeding to administer this sacrament, Father Losa, wishing his friend to receive the last indulgence of the Apostolic See, asked him to mention some sin of his past life, in order that he might give him absolution, since one of the conditions for gaining this, is a true and sincere confession of sin. Gregory answered: "By God's mercy, I find nothing on my conscience that causes me trouble." From this reply the Father gathered that he had never been guilty of any deadly sin, and also that he did not at the moment recollect any deliberate venial sin. He then anointed him with the Holy Unction, which Gregory received with sentiments of the deepest piety, and with the most profound recollection. To give him some little comfort, Father Losa urged him to allow some sheets to be brought for his bed. Gregory gave his consent, saying: "Now that I am anointed, I may allow them." Thinking that the last moment had arrived, the Father said to him: "Will you die now?" Gregory, speaking with himself, said: "Now, nature, wilt thou die?" showing, as it were, pity and compassion for the inferior and sensitive part of his being.

His sufferings were very great, though he gave no voluntary sign of them; yet there was a look of agony in the pale, wan face, that told what his tongue refused to utter. The Father, noticing this, asked him where the pain lay. He replied: "From the crown of my head to the sole of my foot, every part of me is extremely pained." Besides bodily pain, he suffered great mental anguish, for God seems to have left him in the greatest interior desolation. His soul was dry and barren, like earth parched by a scorching sun. There was no sweetness from the Lord. The heavens above him were as brass, and the earth beneath his feet as the flinty rock, so that he might cry out with his dying Saviour: "My God, My God, why hast Thou forsaken Me?" Added to this, he was troubled and grieved for the souls of others. On this head it will be advisable to relate one instance, suppressing, as Father Losa did, for prudential reasons, the names of persons, though, as he says himself, those in Mexico would know who they were, even though no name were mentioned, because of the publicity which the fact afterwards obtained.

It appears that among the people of high degree who came from Mexico to visit Gregory in his last illness, there was a very noble lady, the wife of a gentleman who held a high office in the Government. She was a vain, worldly-minded woman, fond of dress, expensive in her tastes, and passionately fond of gaming. She used to spend whole days playing at cards with other ladies addicted to similar pursuits, and by her high station gave them encouragement to persevere in these evil ways. In spite of all this, she was tender-hearted, and very kind and charitable to the poor. Nearly three weeks before Gregory's death she set out from Mexico for the express purpose of going to Santa Fé to pay him a visit.

Father Losa, hearing of her intention, sent word by a mutual friend, that she was not to put her foot inside the house of one from whose advice she had profited so little. From this it would seem that Gregory had used all his influence to wean her from her scandalous habits, which were a source of the greatest grief to her excellent husband. The messenger carried these words to her, and, meeting her on the road, delivered them to her personally, adding, moreover, that she could not by any possibility gain access to the sick man.

The lady, on her side, was not to be baffled. She sent many messages which needed answers, and this gained time to draw nearer and nearer, till at length, with a woman's pertinacity, she succeeded in compassing her object, for when Father Losa put the matter to Gregory, he said: "She comes with a good desire to amend, and is willing to leave off gaming and idleness; it will therefore be good for her to see me. You may grant her request without fear."

Father Losa then relented, and gave her permission to enter into the house. At the door, one of her sons, who had accompanied her, said to his mother: "Father Losa was determined you should not cross this threshold." She replied: "He was right; but I will amend." She entered the room where Gregory lay, and seeing the pain he was in, her eyes filled with tears, and throwing herself upon her knees by his bedside, she began to do for him some of those little offices, which women's hands alone have the cunning to do well. She set the room in order, she put him in a more easy position upon his wretched bed, she prepared his food and gave it to him, as if she had been his mother. All this time she was earnestly recommending herself to the prayers of the holy man, and begging him with tears to plead for her with God, in order that He might bring about in her soul a thorough conversion of life and manners. Her own earnest entreaties, and Gregory's prayers, soon moved our gracious God to pour His grace into her heart, and effect a thorough reform. She began earnestly to search into herself: she soon had the grace to see herself as God saw her, and, having once seen that picture, she began to hate herself and the life she had been leading. One of the first signs of her conversion was the burning of a pack of cards which she had concealed in her sleeve, and had brought with her to while away the time. The next was, that she went to Father Losa and made a humble confession, which had the effect of completely changing the whole tenor of her life.

After staying a few days with them, she prepared to return to Mexico. Before leaving the house, she turned to Gregory and earnestly begged of him to assist her by his prayers. Then addressing herself to Father Losa, she said with great cheerfulness: "Bear me witness, good Father, that Gregory has promised me, when I die, to come and conduct my soul to heaven, because I know not the way." She then turned to Gregory once more, and said: "Will you promise me this?" He said: "Yes, I promise." After this she bade him farewell, and went to Mexico, a changed woman in life and heart. She had left it with a soul full of worldliness, she returned to it cleansed from her sins, and thoroughly broken of her evil habits.

Two remarkable circumstances occurred before she returned to Mexico after her visit to Santa Fé. The first was that Gregory was almost instantaneously more grievously afflicted with the racking pains which were loosing one by one the slender threads that bound him to this world. The second was, that this lady was afflicted with the same disorder of which Gregory was dying. In spite of the pain and inconvenience occasioned by it, she continued to serve him with great care for two days, ministering to his wants with the tenderness of a mother, and pouring forth by his bedside torrents of repentant tears. Her malady grew hourly worse, and at length compelled her, contrary to her inclination, to relinquish the hope of being able to close Gregory's eyes, when his spirit had fled to its reward. When she came to bid him adieu, after making all preparations for her return to Mexico, Gregory said to her: "Farewell; because, by reason of the weakness of our bodies, we shall see each other no more."

On reaching home, she sent a letter to Father Losa, which convinced him that her soul had been touched by the finger of God, and that her conversion was a change wrought by the hand of the Most High. Many and skilful were the physicians who attended, and did their utmost to heal her; she cared not for them, provided only the physician of her soul would earnestly recommend her to God. Every day she grew worse. The disorder had seized upon, and kept a close grip of her vital powers, and drained the sources of her life. She heeded not the approach of death, but poured forth bitter tears over the past—that misspent time, which might indeed be atoned for, but could never be recalled.

As she drew near her death, Father Losa observed that Gregory's sufferings became greater. When he was thus, as it would seem, at the supreme moment, a Notary arrived from Mexico, bearing a letter from the lady recommending herself to his prayers. He answered the lawyer as one would who was burthened with a great load: "I do so; and her burthen is very heavy upon me." This was the first expression, approaching in any way to the nature of a complaint, that had ever escaped his lips within the memory of Father Losa, and caused him considerable surprise. His friend was not burthened long, for the lady died with sentiments of the deepest contrition for the past, thus atoning, by the edifying manner of her death, for the many scandals of her life.

As soon as the news arrived, Father Losa communicated it to Gregory. His only answer was: "God is powerful." Wishing to learn what he could possibly mean by this, the Father questioned a Brother from the Hospital, who was attending him, and asked if anything extraordinary had happened about the time of the lady's death. He said that he had observed Gregory to be, as it were, out of himself, and in an ecstatic state. From this Father Losa ventures to suggest, that his friend had literally fulfilled his promise to her, and had been present in spirit at her death, in order to assist her in her passage from this world into eternity.

This incident is evidently introduced by the author of Gregory's life to manifest to us the great zeal which the holy man had for the salvation of his neighbour's soul. It was not a zeal of mere words and expressions, such as we oftentimes see in many devout people. This very quickly cools, when something must be done to prove it. Gregory's zeal proved itself by deeds. He was willing to suffer, and, as this case shows, actually did suffer, in order to save that poor frivolous woman. These sufferings did not affect his body only, which ached from head to foot, but pierced into his soul also, and drew from him that cry of anguish: "Jesus, help me! What a purgatory is this!" Words such as these, coming from one usually so silent and self-possessed, showed an amount of agony which it is fearful to think upon.

In the midst of this trial, as Father Losa was about to leave the room, Gregory cried out to him: "Stay with me.." There was a great mystery in the words of Jesus to His Apostles, when He besought them to remain with Him. They indicated without doubt the desolation of our Lord's soul, and by making use of them, the holy man wished his friend to know the barrenness and destitution of spiritual comfort in which God had left him. Yet the courage and constancy with which he endured this trial, plainly pointed him out as a good servant of God, who was content to follow Him, not only in sunshine and prosperity, but in storm and adversity, through rough and rugged ways, where the rock cut his feet, and the thorns tore and lacerated his flesh.

For his own particular edification, Father Losa had the habit, during Gregory's last illness, of asking him various questions, which tested him, and showed whether these ailments in any way interfered with his usual exercises. Accordingly from time to time he used to say to him: "How fares your exercise of the love of God?" Even up to the moment of his death, the invariable answer always was: "Very well." That this was actually the case is evident from his answers to various questions which the good Father put to him. "Does not your pain," said he, "withdraw you in some degree from God?" He said: "Not in the least." Seeing him in great torture on another occasion, he asked: "Is your mind on God now?" He replied at once: "Where else should it be?" When he was in his agony, and close to his end, the Father said: "Do you retain God well in your mind?" "Not ill," he replied. A little later, when he was more calm, he turned to the Father and said: "Perseverance, with peace, is of great value." Father Losa then comforted him, and said: "God is leading you to Himself by the Cross, as He did His own Son." To this Gregory made answer: "I am glad that His Will is being fulfilled in me." Then deeming it time to put the blessed candle in his hand—a custom observed among all Catholics, to remind the dying Christian that his faith ought to burn bright and clear in that supreme moment—Father Losa said: "Will you have the candle?" Gregory replied: "There is no secret with me now; all is as clear as the noonday." By these words he alluded to the story of Don Alonzo XI., who, before breathing his last, said to the bystanders: "Give me the candle; let me go to see this great secret." Shortly after he had received the candle, he calmly and peacefully breathed forth his soul into the hands of God, retaining to the very last moment of his life, the full use of his faculties, and passing gently away from loving God here, to the everlasting enjoyment of Him in heaven. He died in the early morning of Saturday, the twentieth of July, in the year 1596, on which day the Carmelites keep the festival of St. Elias, first father and founder of that solitary life, which Gregory Lopez had observed so faithfully, and loved so well.

He was fifty-four years of age when he died. Of these he had passed thirty-three in solitude. Death wrought no change in his body; he was as if he were alive, and to those who looked upon him, he had the appearance of one resplendent with glory. His body exhaled a delightful odour, which impregnated the very clothes with which he was covered, so that to this day they retain their fragrance. His death was looked upon as one of so great holiness, that the two priests, and some devout laymen who were present, did not dream of praying for him. Their joy, in thinking that he had at length shaken himself loose from the trammels that bound him to the earth, drove all thoughts of sorrow from their minds.

A few days before his death, John de Cervantes, Vicar-General of the Archbishop, and afterwards Bishop of Guaxaca, came to visit him. While in the house, he conferred with Father Losa as to the place where Gregory desired to be buried. The Father told him that Gregory had no particular wish on that point, but had left him to arrange all such matters. "Nevertheless," said he, "I will inform him of the errand upon which you have come, and see what he will say." On hearing the purpose of the Vicar-General's visit, he said at once: "Let what the Vicar wishes be done, for his will is God's Will." On hearing this, the Vicar ordered him to be buried in the church of Santa Fé, but made a proviso that if in after years it should be thought fitting to proceed to his canonization, he should be removed to the Cathedral Church of Mexico. Many of the most eminent persons in Mexico followed Gregory to the grave, testifying by their presence at his funeral, the profound veneration in which they had ever held him.

They brought with them everything requisite for a grand and solemn Requiem. This was celebrated by Alonzo de la Mota, Bishop Elect of Guadalaxara. The body was interred close to the gospel side of the Altar. At his funeral a great concourse of people pressed eagerly round the bier, to touch it, and many tried to cut pieces off the pall which covered the body. All looked upon him as a Saint; all pressed around his mortal remains to do them honour. Thus he who had shunned the society of men, to give himself up wholly to God, drew all men unto him; whereas, those who leave God to serve the world are not unfrequently despised by the very world they so eagerly try to serve.

CHAPTER XII.

SIGNS IN EVIDENCE OF GREGORY'S SANCTITY.

SHORTLY after Gregory's death, a Religious woman, for whose sanctity he had a great esteem, and whose exemplary life entitled her in every way to the friendship of so holy a man, saw him while she was absorbed in prayer. He came near, and addressed her thus: "Sister, I am going to heaven: you shall not go so soon, because your presence is necessary for the service of God, and for the comfort of this Convent." After this he disappeared from her sight, but, like all such blessed visitants, left her soul full of sweetness and holy resignation to the Will of God. Before this she had, like the Apostle, groaned beneath the burthen of the flesh, with all its pains and wearisome miseries, and had desired to be loosed from her prison-house, that she might go to Christ; but now her will was to do and to suffer as long as it should be pleasing to the adorable Will of God. Before any news of his death had reached Mexico, or could possibly have reached it, she said to her confessor: "Gregory Lopez is dead. He has been here himself, and revealed it to me." Her confessor afterwards testified to the truth of this; but at that moment he counselled his penitent not to mention this occurrence to any one, but by more earnest and humble prayer, to beg of God light to know if the vision had come from Him, for "the spirits are to be proved if they be of God." Twelve days afterwards, when Father Losa inquired of her what had occurred at the time of Gregory's death, she revealed the vision to him also, and added, that she had heard, as it were, from the lips of Jesus Himself these words: "Why, think you, is Gregory seated near Me? Because for My sake he abandoned temporal things, and lived with Me in inward recollection and silence."

From another Religious of great virtue, with whose spiritual and interior life the shrewd Father was well pleased, he learnt that, about five years before Gregory's death, she had a vision concerning him.

Being in a weak state of health, she had lain down on her bed after the hour of Prime. A deep sleep came over her, during which she saw the heavens open, and a procession go forth, composed of representatives from all the Religious Orders, and many Martyrs were in their ranks; also the most Holy Virgin, and lastly our Lord Himself, surrounded by His Apostles. This excited great wonder in her soul, and in reply to her question what all this might mean, she was given to understand that they were going to visit and console Gregory Lopez, who was then lying sick, and had not eaten for five days.

A gentleman of great wisdom and piety, who had conceived a special affection for Gregory, went to see him, and recommend himself to his prayers. This was a few days before Gregory's death. The holy man promised that he would not fail to remember him before the throne of God, whenever he should reach the kingdom of heaven. It might perhaps have been a week afterwards, that a vision was granted him wherein he beheld Gregory all resplendent with glory. On seeing this, his heart was filled with spiritual joy, and he praised God, Who is wonderful in His Saints, and then, as it seemed to him, he fell asleep again. From this he was waked by Gregory, whose holy soul seemed to seize upon and pervade his whole person, moving him in an extraordinary manner to praise and bless God, so that he did this without effort, and as it were, in spite of himself.

About ten years before Gregory's death, a very holy servant of God, whose sanctity was so great that he was favoured with frequent ecstasies, related the following incident which befell him in reference to Gregory.

Happening to be suffering from a very grievous illness, which caused him much pain, he began to reflect how holy, how patient, and how self-denying Gregory was, and thus encouraged himself to bear with his own malady, by thinking how much more the devout servant of God suffered without a murmur or a sigh. His thoughts soon brought him, by the aid of God, into the ecstatic state, wherein he beheld represented before his mind's eye, an image, bright as a diamond, and transparent as crystal. "Such," said a voice to him, "is the soul of Gregory Lopez." He afterwards mentioned this vision to Gregory, who neither made any remark to him about what he said, nor ever afterwards mentioned it to any one.

A certain Religious, while praying in choir, received during Divine Office, from God, through the intercession of Gregory, such a clear knowledge of his own nothingness, that the change it wrought in him was wonderful to behold, and conduced very much to the edification of all who knew him. At the same time, so great a love of God was poured into his heart, and that heart was drawn into such a close union with God, that for more than two months he persevered in one continued act of love, without ever once interrupting it.

A hard-working, devout priest, upon whom the sanctity of Gregory had made a great impression, began to reflect within himself on hearing of the holy man's death, how happy his condition was in heaven, and how powerful his prayers before God. While pondering thus, a lively assurance took possession of him, that since he had had the privilege of knowing and conversing with Gregory while on earth, he would now be helped by his prayers in heaven. Shortly after, he heard, or seemed to hear, in his sleep, a voice which said to him: "Ask, ask!" In obedience to this command, he besought God to grant him a favour for which he had often prayed before, but had never been able to obtain it. On the very next day his request was granted, and he affirmed that many other petitions were favourably received by God, and blessings bestowed, not only on himself, but also upon others for whom he prayed, through the intercession of Gregory.

A devout man, who had often consulted Gregory, and received advice from him, desired that, though dead, he would still continue to befriend him. In answer to his petition, he obtained during prayer an internal assurance that his request was granted, and seemed, moreover, to hear within himself a voice which said: "Judge not thy neighbour, and be more temperate."

By these and many other wonderful occurrences, God thought fit to glorify Gregory after his decease, and by them men were taught how great was the sanctity of this poor Solitary, and induced to honour the Giver of all good gifts, Who had deigned to show forth His power in one so lowly and so unpretending.

CHAPTER XIII.

MIRACLES WORKED BY GREGORY'S RELICS.

IT need not be matter of surprise to us, that God should desire to honour His Saints, not only in their heavenly country, but even in the place of their exile. They were His special friends during the days of their mortal life; they lived in close union with Him, and their bodies were the temples in which He delighted to dwell. It is only natural, therefore, to expect that in return for their faithful service, He should be ready to give ear to their prayers, and, through their intercession, work wonders which will redound both to their honour, and to the exaltation of His own ever blessed and holy Name.

In the case of Gregory, these wonders were so great, and their occurrence so frequent, that people ceased to be surprised, and did not take sufficient care to collect and duly record them, otherwise the simple narrative of them would have filled a very considerable volume. However, some of the most authentic and unquestionable have been preserved, and these we shall proceed to lay before the reader. On the day of Gregory's burial, an Indian lady of high rank was present, and came to take a last look at the face of the holy man, whom she had venerated so much during his life. For some time previously she had altogether lost the use of one of her arms, and was unable even then to move it. As she bent down to kiss the hand of the dead man, she felt herself suddenly cured, and was able to move and raise her arm, just as if it had never been injured.

A little girl, aged about five years, had brought upon herself a grievous disease, which she had contracted in consequence of a very singular habit. It appears that she used to eat earth, which, by reason of the obstruction it produced in her stomach, caused her to swell out to an extraordinary size. A malignant fever seized upon her; her head and heart became affected, and she was brought to the very verge of death. The child, addressing the lady under whose care she was living, and who was as much distinguished for her piety as she was for the nobility of her birth, said to her: "Dear lady, apply that relic of the blessed Gregory to me, that I may not die." The lady complied with the wish of the child, and left her. She was then in a burning fever. In the morning, as the lady was going forth, according to her usual custom, to assist at Matins, she called in to see her little protégée. She found her in a sweet and refreshing sleep, quite free from every symptom of her disease.

Being greatly astonished, she awoke her, saying: "My dear child, how are you?" "I am quite well now," said the little one; "your Saint has cured me of my disease."

In Mexico, there was a lady of very high rank, who was troubled with such violent headaches, that it was feared she would lose her reason. Every remedy had been tried, but instead of giving her relief, they seemed rather to augment than to diminish her pain. Having in her possession part of a tunic which had belonged to Gregory, she determined to apply it with great faith for the alleviation of her suffering. She accordingly put it upon her head, and found instantaneous relief.

A young couple belonging to the city of Mexico were in sore distress at the illness of their first and only child, which seemed to be sick beyond all hope of recovery. The well-nigh distracted mother prayed from her almost broken heart, that God would not take her child away. But hour after hour slipped by, and God seemed deaf to her cry. The little sufferer moaned piteously, drooping and fading away like a beautiful flower before the eyes of its despairing parents. At length one of the servants recollected that there was in the house a relic of the blessed Gregory. In all haste this was sought for, and applied to the dying child. The result struck the bystanders with astonishment; for almost the moment after the application was made, the child fell into a gentle sleep, and awoke after a few hours, perfectly restored to health. To their dying hour the grateful parents never ceased to thank God for the mercy He had shown them, through the merits of His servant Gregory.

In the same city of Mexico there was a certain priest who was grievously tormented by the tooth-ache. For three whole days and nights he had not a moment of rest, but the same sharp, racking pain tortured him, till he was almost beside himself. His face was swollen to a great size, and he was faint and weary for want of sleep. His mother brought him a piece of Gregory's garment, which he applied with great faith and piety to his face. In this case, also, the cure was almost instantaneous. The priest fell into a profound sleep, and on awaking next morning found that he was entirely free from pain, and that every trace of the swelling had disappeared.

A gentleman of Mexico, well known in that city, had a slave who met with a very serious accident, by which he was so bruised that people thought he was dead. A lady who happened to be near the place where the accident occurred, had in her possession part of the shirt which Gregory wore when he died. Taking the relic out of the casket in which she carried it, she applied it to the forehead of the poor bruised creature. He immediately recovered his consciousness, and, though greatly torn and wounded, felt perfectly well. Those who saw him asked in surprise if he had no pain. He answered without hesitation: "None whatever." Great was the astonishment of all, and loud their praise of God, Who wrought, through the relics of His servant Gregory, miracles which recalled to their minds the memory of those days when linen cloths which had but touched the Apostle St. Paul had the power to cast out devils, and to raise the dead to life.

In the city De los Angelos, a certain lady, when the time of her delivery drew nigh, was attacked by the measles. Her case was a very sad one, for the child died before it could be brought to the birth, and she herself was reduced to the last extremity by the violence of the disease. Her husband in great grief sent for one of the Brothers from the Hospital, to prepare his wife for the worst. The Brother's name was John Valleio, a man who put great faith in Gregory's intercession. Before leaving the Hospital he took with him a relic of the holy man. On reaching the abode of the gentleman, he found the lady almost at the point of death. But he never lost heart. Taking out this little relic, he applied it to the sick lady's neck. "Be of good heart, Madam," said he, "and trust in God, for His servant Gregory Lopez will obtain your recovery." The lady did as the Brother told her. Putting all her trust in God, and having a firm faith in the efficacy of Gregory's intercession, she lifted up her heart in prayer. In a very short time she was safely delivered, and recovered from her sickness. The same Brother cured another lady in the same city, who was so tortured by racking headaches, that she used to scream out with the pain. He simply applied the relic of Gregory to the affected part, and the pain left her.

In the city of Tlaxcala, a young man was stricken with a frightful leprosy, which covered him from head to foot with one vast sore. He was an object at once of horror and of pity to all who saw him. In vain he tried one physician after another; their prescriptions did him no good. He wearied of his life, and became loathsome even to himself. A Brother from the Hospital bade him try the effect of Gregory's relics, and for this purpose gave him a piece of linen, which had once belonged to him. The poor sufferer took it with great joy, and, as he had been directed, applied it to his neck. He began at once to improve in health; his foul disease began to leave him; his sores dried up; the bad flesh grew sound, and in eight days he was perfectly cured. His gratitude knew no bounds, and he never wearied of publishing the mercies of God to him, through the intercession of Gregory Lopez.

In the village of Hiualpa there lived a gentleman who for more than sixteen months suffered incessantly from colic. The pain occasioned thereby was intense, and at times made him almost beside himself. The wife of the Chief Justice paid him a visit, and seeing the torture he endured, began to speak of the wondrous cures wrought upon those who with faith had begged the intercession of Gregory Lopez. Her narrative filled the poor afflicted man with a great desire to try the efficacy of the Solitary's prayers. The lady gave him a relic, which he applied to the place where he felt most pain. In a short time he was completely cured, and never after suffered any inconvenience from that disorder, which so nearly deprived him of life.

A cure in every respect as wonderful was wrought in the person of Alonzo de la Fuente, a Brother belonging to the Hospital of Convalescents. This man had for six years been living in the hospital of Guasteca, grievously ill of what seemed a species of leprosy. His flesh was full of humours, boils, and running sores, which it seemed impossible to heal. As soon as one was cured, another broke out in some other part of his body, so that he was a pitiable object to look upon. About the time of which we are speaking, he became worse than usual, for two large abscesses, each the size of an egg, began to form, one upon his ankle, the other upon his forehead. The Superior deemed it advisable in his case to try what a change of air would effect. They hoped that if he were removed to a warmer climate, there might possibly be a greater chance of checking his disorder. He was consequently removed to the Hospital of St. John de Uloa, which was on the sea coast. But it turned out that the moisture of the sea air, and the northerly winds which usually prevail there, only made the condition of the poor sufferer worse. He began to be very low-spirited, and to give up all hope of recovery. He sat, as it were, under the very shadow of death, and nought seemed left for him but the grave. At length, plucking up courage, he followed the advice of St. James, and began to pray in the midst of his sadness. A great confidence in the intercession of Gregory, concerning whom he had heard a great deal, began to spring up within him. " I have tried all human aid," said he within himself, " there yet remains the hand of Almighty God." Having in his possession some pieces of linen which had belonged to the holy man, he took them out of the case where he had kept them, and casting off all his bandages, and ointments, and poultices, he applied the simple linen which had belonged to Gregory to the sore places. Wonderful to relate, within three or four days he found himself perfectly cured, and able to walk about, and perform his ordinary duties.

Such are a few of the wonders worked through the intercession of Gregory. There are a vast many more on record, but not being so well authenticated as those we have given, it was thought fit not to mention them. From what has been put before the reader, he will be able to judge of what nature they were. If they serve no other purpose, they will at least bear witness to the high esteem and reputation for heroic sanctity, which Gregory's holy and austere life excited in the hearts of all classes of society, from the simple Indian convert to the Governors and Bishops, who could examine with a calm and critical eye his every look and gesture, and give to them their proper meed of praise or blame.

PART II.

CHAPTER I.

HIS KNOWLEDGE OF SACRED SCRIPTURE.

GREGORY LOPEZ never received what is termed "a liberal education," that is to say, he never went through a collegiate or university course of studies, and consequently did not acquire a knowledge of the learned languages. It is necessary to make this statement in order that the reader may be able to appreciate the wonderful power with which God afterwards endowed him. At the time when he was in the midst of his ascetical career, the reading of the Holy Scripture in the vulgar tongue was forbidden by the ecclesiastical authorities. In this prohibition every right-minded man will perceive the boundless love and reverence of the Catholic Church for the Sacred Text; for the sole reason which prompted this closing of the great Book to the people, was the fear—and the well-grounded fear—lest their faith should be corrupted by the spurious editions which at that time were brought out by different Sects of heretics, who wrested the original to serve their own purposes. When this order was promulgated, Gregory procured the Vulgate edition, which the Church did not forbid to be used, because it is her own approved translation. Though he had never learned Latin, in which the Vulgate is written, he could nevertheless render it into Spanish with wonderful fluency and elegance. Those who at times heard him translating, could not believe that the book he read from was not Spanish. No doubt the similarity of the Latin language to the Spanish might help him much; his previous knowledge acquired by reading the Scripture in the vernacular might help him much, but not, we should imagine, to the extent of enabling him to read it off, as if he had been looking at a book written in his mother tongue. We may therefore attribute his acquaintance with the Latin language in great measure to the infused knowledge which God at times vouchsafes to give to His chosen servants for purposes known to Himself. Owing to the acuteness of Gregory's mind, and to his continual perusal of the Sacred Text, he was able in later years to recite by heart all the historical Books of the Old Testament, the Gospel according to St. Matthew, and that according to St. John, together with those parts of the other Gospels which are omitted by these two Evangelists. He also knew, word for word, St. Paul's Epistles and the Apocalypse of St. John. In fact, he was so well acquainted with the Sacred Books, that when asked about any text in them he could repeat it with great readiness and wonderful accuracy.

Nor was his knowledge confined to a mere verbal acquaintance with the text. He had penetrated, moreover, into its sense, and could explain its various hidden meanings. Of this accuracy, and of his power of interpretation, he gave many proofs during the course of his life, some of which it will be interesting to produce here.

The Vicar-General of the Archdiocese of Mexico, Peter de Pravia, came to the house of Father Losa to visit Gregory, at a time when the latter was recovering from a grievous sickness. In the course of conversation, the Vicar mentioned a passage from Holy Scripture, which he said he had never been able to find. When Gregory had heard it, he said: "That text is not in the Bible at all, but there is one very like it;" and thereupon taking his Bible, he opened it, and laid his finger upon the words he referred to, and Father Pravia found to his astonishment that they were the very words he had been in search of for so long a time.

On another occasion it happened that three Doctors of Divinity, from the Royal University of Mexico, came to the village of Santa Fé for the express purpose of conferring with Gregory upon certain difficulties in the Sacred Text which they could not understand. At the same time they asked him, if there were any passages in Scripture which would prove, or throw any light upon a certain matter which they then mentioned to him. He answered their Scriptural difficulties with such clearness as to fill them with amazement, and then cited a text upon the other matter which they had proposed to him, which was so much to the point that they raised their hands in astonishment, and exclaimed: "This is indeed an able man! What is all our learning compared with his? Blessed is the man whom Thou, O Lord, shalt instruct!"

Whilst conversing one day with some Religious, greatly renowned for their learning, one of them quoted a sentence, as if it had been from Scripture. Gregory at once said to him: "That is not Scripture." Upon this they were greatly astonished, and searched the Bible for it in vain; the passage was nowhere to be found, nor could any text, as in the former case, be discovered which bore any similarity to it.

In fact, he was so well acquainted with Scripture that he could tell exactly how many times some particular word was used, and whether a word was mentioned in any specified passage or not. This was so well known, that a public lecturer on Scripture, a man highly esteemed by Gregory, once said to Father Losa: "I never speak with so much caution on my own particular branch of study, as in the presence of our mutual friend."

Some Prebendaries were one day speaking to him about knowledge of Scripture, and mentioned a man of their acquaintance who knew the whole Psalter by heart. Gregory remarked upon this, that "the thing to be esteemed in cases of this nature was not the simple knowledge itself, but the power to use it when required." In this respect his skill was truly wonderful, for his memory always furnished him with the right words, at the right time, and in the right place.

Several of the great preachers used to retire to Santa Fé to prepare their discourses; and a saying of theirs will give us an idea of Gregory's scriptural proficiency.

In selecting books to aid them in their task, they never took a concordance of the Sacred Text with them, for they used to say: "Where Gregory Lopez is, there is no need of a concordance."

The Archbishop, in the visitation of his Diocese, came to Guasteca, where Gregory was residing. Having a grievous doubt upon a certain matter, he sent Father Losa to Gregory to have it solved. The Father conveyed the prelate's case to him, and it was solved by him with so much clearness and weight of argument, that the good Father, fearing lest he should mar the logical accuracy with which Gregory had answered, told the Archbishop that it were far better to go and hear the solution from the holy man's own mouth. Accordingly, when his business was finished in the city, the Archbishop paid Gregory a visit, and heard the solution of the difficulty from his own lips. In a conversation which he afterwards had with Father Losa on the subject, he expressed himself highly pleased with what he had heard, and seemed deeply impressed with what he had seen. "I never imagined," said he, "that he knew so much."

He seems to have made a similar impression upon the mind of Father Dominic de Salazar, a celebrated Dominican preacher. Once after holding a conference with him, he was so amazed at the learning, the depth of mind, the grasp of principles and the many-sided knowledge which he displayed, that he cried out in the presence of three of the most learned men of his Order: "Look, Fathers, at this wonder! we, after long years of study, are mere children in knowledge, compared with this young man!"

He simply filled many of the learned who came to visit him, with amazement; for he unravelled for them the most knotty questions, and followed out the most intricate arguments, till putting his finger upon the cleverly-concealed fallacy, he crushed it by the force of his reason; and then put forward his own view with such clearness and brevity, that what he advanced could neither be misunderstood nor refuted. Among others, there came a certain Doctor of Divinity, who had a few days before assisted at the public disputations in the Jesuits' College at Mexico. These were principally upon that text of Malachy: "Behold, I send My Angel before thy face." The Doctor, out of curiosity, asked Gregory the meaning of it, and received in answer so many and such curious expositions upon the passage, that he declared he had not heard so lucid an explanation, nor one so well expressed, in the whole defence set up by some of the highest intellects in the country, as he that day received from the lips of Gregory Lopez.

CHAPTER II.

HIS SPIRITUAL DISCERNMENT.

IT was God's Will that His servant Gregory should be endowed, not only with intellectual power, but also with that keenness of vision which penetrates into the hearts, and searches the souls of men.

He gave so many proofs of this, that the good Father, whose privilege it was to share the same roof, and live with him on terms of the closest intimacy, did not hesitate to declare it to be his firm belief, that Gregory could discern the soul with the eye of his spirit, as clearly as he did his own body with the eye of the flesh. This discernment of spirits is one of those gifts mentioned by St. Paul as proceeding from the Holy Ghost, and is a power very requisite for a spiritual man. For not every thought, nor impulse is to be attended to or obeyed; they must be searched, to see if they be from God. Very many, indeed, proceed from nature; many from grace. To be able to discern what is merely natural, from that which is the effect of God's grace, conduces much to advance a man in the way of perfection, and is consequently of great importance to one who would lead a spiritual life. Gregory possessed this gift and used it, not only for his own advantage, but also for the good of all those who came to consult him.

Father Losa gives the first instance of this power of penetration into the souls of others, as having happened to himself. For several months he had confined himself almost exclusively to discursive meditation, and had found in it nought but dryness and affliction of spirit. His soul seemed to him like earth that has been parched under a scorching sun. All love or aspiration after God, and every emotion of generosity, had apparently died out of his heart. He was filled with desolation, and sighed in vain for the days that were gone, when the lamp of God shone over his head, and his Creator dwelt secretly with him in his tabernacle. In the midst of this dryness, duty called him forth upon some errand of charity. On the way to perform it, the dew of God's grace fell abundantly upon his thirsty soul, and what was but a few moments before a barren desert, became, as it were, suddenly, a very garden of delights. A most sweet and heavenly joy took possession of him; the fountain of prayer welled up within him, and rose spontaneously, without any effort on his part. He was inebriated with such delight, that he thought himself in heaven.

On his return, he related to Gregory what had befallen him whilst on his errand of mercy, remarking: "My soul was enlarged within me." "Say rather," replied Gregory, "that nature enlarged herself within thee." Father Losa did not quite apprehend the entire meaning of these words at the moment, but reflecting upon them afterwards at his leisure, the truth hidden in them dawned upon him, and threw a flood of light upon his mind, which brought plainly to his view the vast difference between nature and grace. He had been accustomed all his life-long, as vicar of a large parish, to be busied in external works of charity. These works, though in themselves very meritorious, have the property of recreating and satisfying our human nature, and oftentimes self-love intermixes itself with the very best of them, so that in the execution of them, it not unfrequently happens, that we seek ourselves,—our own gratification and benefit, rather than the glory of God, or the good of our neighbour, purely and simply. But in the exercise of meditation to which he had betaken himself, there was nothing to recreate or amuse the senses; nature was, so to speak, upon the rack. Everything that could afford it pleasure was withdrawn. The mind and heart, abstracted from all things without, were centred upon God, or at least were striving to be so centred upon Him. Now when the good Father left off this exercise, when he unbent the bow, so to speak, and walked abroad to perform his duty, in which external things would help him to feel glad; when he looked round him upon the gorgeous scenery of that luxurious climate, and saw the lofty mountains, and the green gardens and fields; when he heard the woods resounding with the cries of gaudily plumed birds, and the air filled with the hum of the myriad insect life, his heart expanded within him, because he had taken off all restraint, and his nature was filled with a quiet happiness which he mistook for the effect of grace. However, on his return when he again betook himself to his mental exercises, confident of being able to perform them with greater ease, he discovered that nature was stronger within him even than before, and held him chained down to sensible things. By this he perceived that the peace and joy he had experienced, were rather the result of a natural cause, than the effect of the operation of divine grace. The words of Gregory then flashed upon him in the full force of their meaning, and he understood them perfectly. Some Religious called in one day to visit him, and in the course of conversation, it chanced that they mentioned some of the various means which aid men to pray well. One gave it as his opinion, that music was one of the most powerful of these. "I happened," said he, "to be in the Cathedral at Mexico during a great ecclesiastical function, and the sweet and powerful strains of harmony that burst from the choir, and rolled through the vast edifice in wave upon wave of thrilling sound, produced so marvellous an effect upon me, that my spirit was stirred within me. Never in my life before did I pray with so much earnestness, peace, and profound quiet, as then." "For my part," said another, "I never pray so well, or with more ease, than when I kneel in choir, surrounded by my brethren, whose good example and presence move me to pray with fervour and devotion. In my own cell I should be dry and distracted, and make a very unsatisfactory sort of prayer altogether." During the conversation, Gregory made no remark whatever to enlighten them, though he could have set them right on these matters by a very few words. It was nature, after all, which in these men was pleased and delighted; one by the sounds which affected and soothed his senses; the other by the presence of those whose goodwill and praise he was anxious to obtain. After the departure of these guests, Father Losa asked him why he had not set them right, and given them advice and instruction in these matters. "Because," replied Gregory, "had I spoken, I should only have been a hindrance, and not a help to them. With that staff of sensible comfort they make some little onward progress, without it they would stand still."

With regard to words and thoughts, God had also bestowed upon him a wonderful keenness of vision, to distinguish those which proceeded from nature, from those which were the effect of divine grace. He used often to say: "Many speak of God, not out of love of Him, but of themselves. Besides the love of God does not consist of words—it is all works,—and is often dumb." Hence we may see the reason why he was so sparing of his words. Having the faculty of discerning when these proceeded from nature and when from grace, he carefully prohibited his tongue from uttering what was a mere outpouring of nature seeking its own ease, and spoke only when what he said came from the Holy Spirit, and would conduce to the edification of others.

To this interior light ever abiding in his soul must be attributed the fact, that he was never troubled with scruples of conscience, but always enjoyed peace and tranquillity of soul.

In matters of faith also, though tempted like other men, he yet never had any doubt; so that at his death when Father Losa, putting the blessed candle into his hand, said: "Wilt thou have this light to see the great secret?" he replied: "There is no secret with me. All is clear as at noon-day." By these words he did not mean that there was no obscurity in his faith, but that in all matters pertaining thereunto he had not the slightest doubt. For faith, as we know, necessarily implies that there is obscurity as to *how* such and such dogmas are so, but not as to the fact that they *are* so. In that respect it leaves us in the most unshaken certainty. This certainty, however, does not take away the obscurity in which these facts are involved, nor the captivity of our reason which consents to receive them thus enveloped in clouds. In this way does God will that we should walk during this life—" Captivating our understandings in His service," as the Apostle speaketh.

From these and many other examples, which shall presently be laid before the reader, Father Losa was emboldened one day, about five years before Gregory's death, to put this categorical question to him: "Do you, or do you not, see the souls of other men; that is to say, do you see their thoughts?"

Gregory answered in his own straightforward way: "I do not." But the good Father, with the daily recurring instances before his eyes of this supernatural power, tells us, that while he was thoroughly convinced of Gregory's scrupulous love for truth, he yet could not but believe that he possessed the gift of seeing into the souls of others, and reading them as we read a book. He gets over the difficulty of the holy man's denial in this way: " Either God had not conferred this gift upon him at the time when I asked him, but did so later on in life; or at the time when I put the question, he did not see them, since this power is not habitual and permanent, but actual like prophecy; that is to say, given only on particular occasions." However, be that as it may, here are some of the instances recorded, from which the reader will be able to judge for himself. If they do not inspire others with the same firm conviction, as they seem to have imparted to Father Losa, they will at least serve to show that Gregory possessed an acuteness of perception, and a knowledge of the human heart, such as is acquired only by men whose intellect is of the very highest order.

A certain gentleman, who was grievously tempted against faith, came to consult Gregory, while labouring under this torturing trial. He gave him an account of his state, and how he acted in time of temptation. Though often in doubt about his perfect resistance to the subtle difficulties suggested by the devil, he nevertheless could not find that he had wilfully given his consent in any particular instance, and therefore had never mentioned them in confession. "Be not so sure of your fidelity," said Gregory, "for in very truth you have proved yourself a weak soldier." The gentleman, in some trepidation at this answer, said to him: "Well, if you think fit, I will mention them in confession." Gregory then said: "I do not say that you have been guilty of grievous sin in any of these points, but you did not perfectly resist. To have acted as you ought, you should have done so and so," mentioning the precise line of conduct he should have followed. This gentleman inferred from what Gregory told him, that he had seen into his very soul, and he was enabled by following his advice to put to flight all suggestions from the evil one.

A priest, troubled with very serious scruples of conscience, came from a great distance to expose them to Gregory, and to solicit his advice. That advice was so much to the point, that the priest, in great joy, not unmixed with wonder, exclaimed: "You have told me the very things I thought of asking, in which, indeed, I stood in great need of advice." Gregory's words to him are remarkable, if we wish to follow Father Losa's opinion: "God, seeing your necessity, moved me to tell you what you have heard."

There was a certain lawyer, a married man, who afterwards became a Religious, perhaps in reward for the holy life he led even when mixed up in the perilous affairs of his profession. This man went on one occasion, in company with a friend, to visit Gregory. On the way, the lawyer spoke to his friend about matters pertaining to his own soul. They were matters about which Gregory could not possibly, by any natural means, have had any knowledge. Yet the gentleman affirmed, that as soon as he and his friend were presented to the holy man, and before they had mentioned the purpose of their visit,—before they had even put a question to him, he began to discourse to them upon the very matters about which they had been talking, solving each difficulty, and making everything as clear to them as the noon-day. They were so startled that they looked at each other in amazement, and then gave thanks to God for having answered their difficulties before they had proposed them for solution. Ever after, this lawyer took care, when going to visit Gregory, first to examine his conscience, and make all things straight, being thoroughly convinced that it lay open before him; for on all occasions when, after his first visit, he went to ask counsel of him, Gregory used to answer the very question he had come to ask, without waiting for him to propose it.

A Religious, eminent for his great spirituality, and very intimate with Gregory, came to him for the solution of some doubts which caused him much annoyance. As it was night-fall when he arrived, Gregory bade him go to rest and defer their conference till the following day. During the night, the Religious had an internal answer from God, which cleared up the doubts under which he had been for some days labouring, and, at the same time, he felt himself rebuked for coming to seek counsel from a creature, when he might, if he had disposed himself aright, have had the same light granted to him by the Creator. In the morning he presented himself, notwithstanding, before Gregory, intending to tell him everything that had occurred. He was met by him with a smiling countenance, and as the poor man tried to tell him his doubts and the manner in which they had been cleared away, Gregory helped him out with his narration, and then said: " But were you not also reprehended for coming to a creature for advice?" "Yes," he replied, " I had a severe rebuke!" The question filled him with amazement, since it showed him that Gregory had seen, in the light of God's countenance, all that had passed within him.

A priest, much given to the practices of a spiritual life, came to visit Gregory, and remained with him for a fortnight. His observation of the servant of God during that time, led him to believe that he could see all that was passing in the minds of men with whom he conversed. Gregory, of course, never told him that this was the case, but he inferred it from his ordinary conversation, and especially from a remark which he once made to him. This priest had, it seems, received extraordinary favours from God, and had unhappily been somewhat elated by them. He did not mention this to Gregory, but the servant of God, in one of their familiar conferences, looking at him, said: "We aim at being great, but we may take it for a certainty, that either here or hereafter, we shall pay for our lack of humility."

A layman of great piety, very devout to our Blessed Lady, acquired such a degree of sanctity by the fervent recitation of the Rosary, that for some years he was almost always in a state of continual prayer. Seeing that he was so far advanced in mental prayer, he consulted Gregory, to know if it would not be more profitable for him to leave off the Rosary, and apply himself exclusively to the prayer of meditation.

Gregory, who was himself a devoted servant of Mary, knowing very well how great a help the Rosary is to beginners, and what progress it enables them to make in the spiritual life, gave him the simple answer,—No! without assigning any reason whatever for his decision. Acting upon this, the man continued his pious practice for another year. But perceiving at the end of that time that the favours granted to him by God went on daily increasing, and that now he was far advanced in the way of perfection, he determined, without consulting Gregory, to lay aside the Rosary and apply himself to meditation. He did so, and after two or three days found himself encompassed by troubles, and felt his soul parched up with spiritual dryness. In fact, he became incapable of praying at all. This is the danger to which they expose themselves, who think to sail prosperously in the spiritual life without Mary, the Star of the Sea, as their guide. In his grief, he once more betook himself to Gregory and told him of the cross which God had sent him, without, however, mentioning what he knew in his own heart was the most probable cause. Gregory heard him with patience, and then, smiling at him, said: "My good friend, fall to your beads again." He followed the advice given to him, and soon regained his former peace and fervour. He then redoubled his devotion to the Blessed Virgin, and ever after marvelled how Gregory, without hearing a word from him upon the matter, had laid his finger upon the cause of his spiritual aridity.

At times it would happen that seven or more persons would arrive on the same day, and at about the same hour, to hold conferences with him on their spiritual affairs, and to have their doubts solved, or their fears dissipated. They did not meet together on these occasions by any fixed design or previous appointment, nor had Gregory any intimation beforehand of their intended visit; nevertheless, he would often, after admitting them all together into his little room, address to them a short homily, in which each one found that his difficulty was answered, though he had not given the holy man the slightest hint of his troubles. His words to the sorrowful and afflicted were like flashes of light which dispelled the gloom hanging over their souls, and enabled them to see and to lay hold of that which grieved them, or was a hindrance to their spiritual progress. Hence all who came to visit him went away satisfied, with their hearts full of burning desires to do great things for Almighty God.

To a man weighed down with grief who came to him for counsel, he merely said these words: "This is a Purgatory where God detains you;" and they sufficed to comfort and restore quiet to his afflicted soul.

He consoled a priest who was in great affliction, by quoting these words of the Apocalypse: "I counsel thee to buy of me gold, fire-tried, that thou mayest be rich."

Another priest, wearied almost unto death by continual temptations, felt great consolation on hearing Gregory say: "The kingdom of heaven suffereth violence, and the violent alone bear it away."

All classes of society went out to ask him what they should do to be saved, just as the Jews did in the days of St. John the Baptist. To Knights and persons of distinction he said: "Do what you do for the love of God, and that is enough."

To lawyers, judges, and men of business, he used to say: "Change your intentions and you will do much."

Father Losa, who lived with him as a familiar friend, and all those who had even a chance acquaintance with him, could not fail to notice how he spiritualized every thought that passed through his mind, and every word which he might hear from others. A few examples will suffice to show what we mean. If at meals any one made any remark upon the food, as people sometimes will, just to keep the conversation from flagging, and said: "The bread of Santa Fé is good;" Gregory would say: "Yes, sir, it is indeed;" but he would mean the most Holy Sacrament of the Altar, the true Bread of our Santa Fé, or holy Faith.

No one could fail to admire the beautiful flowers which grow in such luxuriance round Santa Fé. Their delicious perfume, their richness, and the splendour of their colours, was the theme of every one's conversation when they first beheld them.

Every expression used by those who talked to Gregory on this subject, was made by him to signify the Saints, whose holiness had its origin from the faith, for without it, it would be impossible to please God. The beautiful springs which poured forth their waters, and formed streams of sparkling brightness which flowed into Mexico, was another topic on which visitors never failed to descant, and say that water was nowhere better than at Santa Fé. Gregory would nod assent to this, meaning by the springs of Santa Fé, God, in Whom the waters of wisdom are the best, and the man who receives them direct from God, has them purer and more wholesome than those which pass through the human understanding. If in speaking of others, any one remarked that they were of a very noble family, he would consider that true nobility consists in being a son of God in spirit. If any one said such or such a lord is a grandee of Spain, he would say to himself: "True greatness consists in being the friend of God, in hearing His divine words, and doing great things in His service." Whenever anything occurred out of which others would think it hard to draw anything spiritual, Father Losa would ask Gregory to do so, and never failed to obtain an answer which would surprise him by its aptitude to the circumstance of the time and place. For example: while some visitors were with him one day, one of those dust storms, which are matters of ordinary occurrence in some parts of the tropics, rose at Santa Fé, where such things rarely happened. On seeing the great columns of dust go whirling and eddying past, some one present remarked: "Oh, you have dust also at Santa Fé, I perceive." Father Losa, noticing the remark, and wondering how it could be spiritualized, said to Gregory: "How can it be that there is dust in Santa Fé?" "Be sure," said Gregory, "there are Saints who live in Santa Fé, who have not yet reached the four and twenty degrees of perfection, and therefore have some dust of the earth still adhering to them; for a man perfectly spiritual is all spirit."

CHAPTER III.

HIS KNOWLEDGE OF HISTORY, SACRED AND PROFANE.

THE fame which Gregory acquired by the holiness of his life, naturally enough attracted much attention, and filled the minds of all who heard of his wondrous ways with the desire to see him, and judge for themselves. Among the number of those who obeyed this impulse there were, no doubt, many who were ready to believe any report about him, no matter how extravagant, and to exaggerate still more what might fall under their own observation. But then, again, there were others who made it their business to see and examine him,—men of cultivated minds, in whom the critical faculty had been highly developed, both by the system of education upon which they had been trained, and by the occupations of their every-day life,—and to their testimony we may yield the most unbounded faith. For their spotless integrity made them as incapable of fostering a lie, as their habit of thought guarded them against swallowing down the marvellous with open-mouthed credulity. Such were John Cobos, of the Order of St. Dominic, a Lector in Theology; Michael de Talavera, Provincial of the Order of St. Francis; and Emanuel de Reynoso, another Franciscan. John Cobos, after a long conference with Gregory, said that, great as was the fame he enjoyed, personal acquaintance with him rather increased than diminished it. He was so captivated by his brilliant parts and profound knowledge, that he begged from him an explanation of the Apocalypse. Gregory complied with the Father's request, and in due time sent him the desired exposition. It was a first copy, and yet it was written with as much neatness as if it had been printed, not a single blot or erasure being visible throughout its entire length.

The Franciscan Provincial, after his interview with

the servant of God, never ceased thanking the Lord for the great favour he had received, in being privileged to speak with one so holy, so humble, and so absorbed in divine contemplation. The other disciple of St. Francis seems to have severely tested Gregory's knowledge of Holy Scripture, for he afterwards used to relate, how he had taken him at random through the entire Bible, proposing one passage from one book, another from another, but found that his answers were always quite correct, and expressed in language most clear and intelligible. Some of the passages selected to test his knowledge, were among the most obscure and difficult to be found in Holy Writ; nevertheless, he explained them all in their literal sense with so great learning, that the Father looked upon him as a second St. Jerome. Another Religious, on hearing this, went to Gregory with several very great and well-known scriptural difficulties. He, too, found that there had been no exaggeration in the estimate of his powers made by the Franciscan.

His knowledge of history, sacred and profane, was at once extensive and accurate. As far as could be gathered from Scripture, he knew all that had passed from the creation of the world till Noah. By this we do not mean that he could simply narrate the events which had occurred during that period, but that he had an intimate knowledge of all the chief characters who had played any notable part in human affairs during those ages. He could go through their pedigrees, and trace their descent, and show how they were related one with another, and what they did, and what they suffered, with as much ease as if he were reading it off a book. His information about the manners and customs, the employments and the inventions, of the men of that period, was also very accurate.

His knowledge of events, and of the men who took part in them, from Noah to Christ, was of a similar nature; so that, when he spoke on these matters, he talked of them as if he had seen them with his own eyes. Of the nations, external to the family of the Sons of God, his information was large and varied. Making the history of the chosen race the centre, round which all other histories turned, he had learnt all about the nations with which they had in any way come in contact. He knew all the incidents of their wars and of their policy, not only with the people of God, but also with each other. He knew by heart all the prophecies, and could point out or recite every passage which related to the birth, the infancy, the childhood, and the youth of our Blessed Lord. Also all such prophecies as had any reference to His preaching, His death, or to the mysteries of our Faith, and the pre-eminence of the law of grace above that of nature, were ready at his command, and could be cited by him most opportunely on all occasions. From the Apostolic Age down to the days in which Gregory himself lived, there was nothing that had occurred, and had been recounted in the historical books of his time, with which he was not intimately acquainted, and about which he did not speak with as much accuracy as if he had been present, and taken part in the actions of which they treated. To begin with the Apostles and their immediate disciples: he knew the history of each one of them, the countries where they preached, and the success of their missions. Of the Popes who sat in St. Peter's Chair till the days of Sylvester, he could recount the respective lives, and the details of the martyrdom by which they sealed their holy and laborious career. The acts of the principal Martyrs who suffered during the persecutions of the Roman Emperors were also at his command. He knew the history of all the Religious Orders, the lives of their founders, and the laws whereby they ruled their followers and guided them to perfection. The heresies which had arisen in the Church, from its foundation till his own day, were accurately known by him, together with the champions of the faith, whom God raised up to combat error, and the Councils in which their various fantastic notions were condemned. He discoursed very learnedly upon the Apocalypse, and particularly upon those passages where mention is made of the Beast, which, he said, was pagan Rome. His study of this part of Scripture caused him to become acquainted with the history of the great Empire, which he could trace from its first beginning to its final overthrow by the Barbarians. From this point he could take up the chronicle of the nations which had worked its ruin, down to the reign of Philip II., the Catholic King of Spain, in whose time he himself was living.

He was very deeply read in all that concerned the origin and progress of Mohammedanism; nor was his knowledge of the countries possessed by those who followed the teaching of its false prophet, by any means slight or superficial. Profane history and pagan mythology were, to use a familiar expression, at his finger ends. Especially was he well versed in that portion of history which treated of the conversion of the various nations to the Faith. He could tell when, by whom, and with what success, the message from God had been brought to the nations sitting in darkness and in the shadow of death. Of all this historical lore, he had made a sort of compilation, beginning with the creation of the world, and carrying it down to his own day. This work was written with so much brevity and exactness, the facts mentioned were so notable, and their accuracy so thoroughly to be relied upon, that many learned men begged Father Losa to grant them permission to make copies of it for their own use.

In addition to this, he had extracted from the various histories he had read, all that could be learnt concerning the faith of different nations, the laws by which they were ruled, and the manners and customs of their peoples. He had thrown this vast accumulation of knowledge into a sort of calendar for every day in the year, something after the fashion of such works as the "Book of Days," and like the wise householder, who could bring forth from his treasure old things and new, he used to amuse his visitors and Father Losa, by reciting to them the curious and valuable information which he had gathered together.

CHAPTER IV.

HIS KNOWLEDGE OF OTHER SCIENCES.

MOST people would be led to imagine, that a man like Gregory Lopez could have but a very scanty store of knowledge, outside of scriptural subjects, and matters pertaining to moral and mystical theology. Their surmise would probably be correct in the case of most of those who give themselves up to the exercises of a spiritual life. But with this great servant of God it was not so. His love for His Master taught him to search into the works of His hands, and to study and admire them, in order to be able to draw thence matter for prayer and praise. We find him, therefore, well acquainted with astronomy, cosmography, and the science of geography. So exact was his knowledge in these matters, and so well skilled was he in everything pertaining to them, that he had, with his own hands, constructed a globe, and drawn up a map, to aid himself in the prosecution of these studies. Those who knew what mathematical nicety was required for the construction of such objects, admired his handiwork very much, and pronounced it correct in every particular. Nor was his geographical knowledge limited to an acquaintance with those countries only, about which it was natural that he should have acquired a certain amount of information; it extended to the whole earth, and when questions were put to him about the most obscure and distant places, he answered them with as much ease and readiness, as if they had been situated in the environs of Mexico or of Santa Fé.

He quite astonished Father Losa by his intimate acquaintance with the anatomy of the human frame, and used to edify him at times, by pointing out the admirable wisdom and goodness of God, displayed in the wondrous conformation of the human body, that masterpiece of God's creative hand, at least in the material world.

No Doctor with a diploma from the Faculty of medicine, was more expert in the healing art than he, or had a deeper insight into the maladies of the human frame. A proof of this was shown by the publication of a medical work, compiled by him for the use of the labouring classes. The prescriptions given therein were of the simplest nature, and admirably adapted for the poor, as containing nothing but what they could easily procure, and that too at very little expense. Their highest commendation, however, was that they ordinarily effected the cure they were destined to operate; an excellence which cannot be found in most medical prescriptions. This healing power was attributed by many, rather to the holiness of the man who prescribed, than to the efficacy of the medicines themselves. By others it was looked upon, partly as the result of Gregory's natural sagacity, and partly as the outcome of that medical science he had somehow or other acquired, and by which he had been taught to select remedies most suitable to expel the diseases for which he undertook to treat. But to whatever cause we may assign this healing power, the fact of its existence is indisputable.

Much is said at the present day about scientific farming and gardening, and many would no doubt think, that more than two centuries ago, such men as peopled the Spanish colonies would never have dreamt it possible to apply science to agriculture. Possibly this was true of the majority of the colonists, but not of Gregory; for Father Losa mentions "his profound knowledge of all herbs," and speaks of his "mixing certain liquids, and giving them as a drink to various kinds of plants, by which they were so changed and so much improved, that who ate of them would scarcely believe they were the same as those cultivated by other men." Gregory would have told this secret to any good and pious Christian, but he feared to disclose it to the world at large, lest some might be induced by their evil passions to pervert their knowledge, and use it to poison plants, and render them mischievous to others, and perhaps destructive of human life.

The good Father in his admiration for Gregory, deems it fitting to record everything in which he surpassed ordinary men. Hence we have him gravely recounting the excellence of his penmanship, which it appears was of a very high order, and executed with so much neatness that it might have been mistaken for print.

Moreover, he expatiates with equal gravity upon the skill he had acquired in making his own clothes, being able to fit himself as well as any tailor. It seems, however, that he could not manage to make his shoes or his hat, but had to content himself with mending the former, till scarcely an inch of the original pair remained, and was obliged to trust for the latter to the charity of his friends. The possession of so many accomplishments might be looked upon rather as hindrances, than as helps to perfection, and of this Father Losa seems to have been somewhat afraid; for he tells us that he once put this very question to his friend Gregory, who replied that his principal aim in all he did, or was able to do, was simply to please his Almighty Lord and Creator, and that by this means he found God in everything.

The rapidity with which he could read a book was very remarkable. On one occasion, for instance, he took up a certain book and read it through in the space of ten hours. At the end of that time, he had completely mastered its contents, and we are assured by those who knew of this fact, that to have done the same, would have cost an ordinary reader an entire month of close and unwearied application. Some will say, that any one possessed of a keen intellect, aided by a quick and retentive memory, could have done as much, for, to a man so endowed, the mere titles of the chapters are oftentimes sufficient to convey a very good notion of their contents. This solution would perhaps hold good in the case of certain classes of books, whose subject-matter is not very deep; but we should imagine it would not be of any great value in the case of such books as the works of St. Theresa, which he read through in less than a day. Yet few men, even among those who had given much time and labour to the mastering of those same works, knew more about them than Gregory. He was afterwards frequently tested upon this point, because people were curious to see if he could have noticed, so as to retain, after such rapid reading, certain minutiæ, mentioned in various portions of the text. To their surprise he remembered everything in the book. Nothing in its pages could be mentioned which he did not know, as accurately as if he had carefully committed it to memory. Furthermore, when asked about any particular portion of it, he could take up the text at the place spoken of, and go on with it, as fluently as if he were reading it from the book. From this we may judge of his intellectual power, of the quickness of his apprehension, and of the tenacious grasp of his memory. In fact, this latter was so vice-like in retaining what it had once laid hold of, that we may readily believe him when he says, that he never forgot anything which he took pains to commit to its faithful keeping.

It will not be out of place here, to give the reader some notion of Gregory's personal appearance. In stature he was far above the middle height, and in every respect fairly proportioned. Yet he was rather slenderly made than of a robust complexion, and towards the end of his life became a mere skeleton, like St. Jerome, St. Basil, and others.

His skin was very white and fair; his hair, eyebrows, and beard, of a hazel colour. His face was long and thin, his forehead broad, high, and projecting. His mouth small, the lips thin and compressed, the under one somewhat protruding. His ears were very small, a feature regarded by many as one of the great signs of noble descent. His eyes were dark, sparkling, and wonderfully keen of vision. His nose small, his teeth white as ivory. Altogether, he was an extremely handsome man. No one could look upon his composed and modest exterior, without forming a very high idea of the beauty of his soul, and feeling themselves spurred on to imitate his austere and spotless life.

Such was the man, who, at little more than twenty years of age, turned his back upon a brilliant career at home, and going to the Indies, hid himself among a savage people. He renounced all that high birth and a splendid intellect might have won for him, and chose a life of obscurity and poverty, in order to serve his Lord and Master with more fervour and entire self-immolation. He succeeded in accomplishing this so effectually, that though many watched him most closely, they could never detect the slightest imperfection in any of his words or actions.

CHAPTER V.

GOVERNMENT OF THE TONGUE.

"IF any man," says St. James, "offend not in word, the same is a perfect man." The same Apostle declares that a man's Religion is vain, if he knows not how to put a bridle upon that slippery member, upon that "world of iniquity," as he calls it. This then is the test of true holiness given by one upon whom we may rely. He was the mouth-piece of the Holy Spirit, and his words have consequently the impress of Eternal Truth upon them. If we judge Gregory by them, we may confidently point to him, and say: "Here is a perfect man,—an Israelite, indeed, in whom there is no guile." For eighteen years that good priest, to whom we owe the narrative of his life, was his constant and devoted companion. From his remarks, we can see that he was a shrewd, sensible man; a man not easily moved to enthusiasm, nor given to emotional outbursts. He had a keen eye for searching out defects, and no friendship could blind him to defects when he saw them. Besides this, he had not chosen Gregory for his master and guide, without being warned, by men as cautious as himself, that he might be deceived; consequently, his eyes were ever open to detect the slightest deviation from what was right, even in the most trivial matters—such as ordinary Christians would never notice at all. Yet, during the whole of that lengthy period, he never heard one word fall from the lips of Gregory, which the most delicate and critical conscience could reprehend. He never spoke a harsh or injurious word against any man. Even when speaking of heresies and of heretics, though he strongly, and with great weight of reason condemned the errors and sins of which they were guilty, he never revealed their names, and always treated them personally with considerate gentleness.

Like most great servants of God, he did not escape the shafts of malignant detractors. Yet, even on occasions when the little things said of him were detailed, as they usually are, by some one who deems himself a friend, his tongue was so completely under his control, or, rather, his heart, from whose abundance the mouth speaketh, was so schooled in virtue, that no querulous or sharp word escaped his lips. His usual remark was: "The person who said that, said it with a good intention." Then he defended the person of his detractor, and gave such a colouring to the fact of his detraction, as completely to screen him from the resentment of his own friends.

A very intimate friend of Gregory's—a man who entertained the very highest opinion of his prudence, virtue, and sanctity—persuaded one of the bishops, when he was about to pass through the Marquisate of Vallé, very near the abode of the holy man, to pay him a visit. His Lordship promised to do so without fail, and kept his promise. Gregory, when apprised of his approach, came out in all humility and reverence to welcome him, and led him into his modest room. When the Bishop's party was seated, the conversation turned upon the most general and ordinary topics of the day, very likely upon the weather, the crops, the working of the mines, and subjects of that nature. Gregory spoke not a syllable during the time the visit lasted, which was upwards of a quarter of an hour. At length the Bishop and his suite took their leave and went on their journey. Gregory's friend was very anxious to know what impression had been made upon his Lordship by this interview, and took the first opportunity of asking him. He was rather taken aback when the Bishop told him "that

Gregory seemed to him to be a senseless fool." "He sat there," said he, "without having once opened his mouth to make a remark, just like a man who had not an idea in his head, nor the ability to give an idea upon the opinions of other men." "But," said the astonished gentleman, "you surely must not have spoken to him upon spiritual things!" "No," said the Bishop, "the conversation turned upon ordinary matters, from which, had he a grain of sense or the least tact, he might have led it to those topics in which he particularly excels." "In that case, then," said Gregory's friend, "I am not at all surprised; because he never speaks unless he is first asked some question, and I am sure he would never speak for the purpose of displaying what he knew." The Bishop's opinion was of course told to Gregory. He rejoiced at the humiliation heaped upon him, and said: "Had I seen a man like myself, I, too, should have been of the same opinion."

In this government of the tongue, he aimed at the repression even of such words as are called "idle." By these we do not mean what are commonly looked upon as such, by a certain class of men, who designate by the mild term of "rude language" what, not unfrequently, borders very closely upon the indecent. Every speech of that kind was entirely banished from a life like Gregory's. But taking an idle word in the signification in which it is understood by Divines, as something superfluous, or useless, we are given to understand that his conversation was entirely free, even from such slight blemishes as would be contracted by the use of an unnecessary expression. Thus, in the beginning of his solitary life, when he was accustomed to look upon the face of nature, if he beheld the heavens, studded with countless brilliant stars, or admired their deep azure blue, or gazed upon pleasant scenery, diversified by rock and wood and stream; he did not, as other people would have done, express his admiration in extravagant epithets, or deal in useless superlatives, but compressed what he had to say, till it became as brief and pointed as an epigram.

There was another way in which he showed his complete control over the tongue, and we might add, over self also. This was when he found himself, as he frequently did, in the company of learned and scientific men. Their conversation often enough turned upon the branches of learning in which they were most skilled. Yet, though as well versed as any of the company in the subject-matter which might happen to be under consideration, he sat there as silent as if he had been an ignorant clown. But if any one asked him for his opinion, he would, in a few appropriate words, flash out a stream of light upon the subject, which served to give them all a glimpse of the vast treasures of wisdom which he possessed.

This was so well known that Don Pedro Agurto, Bishop of Cibu, in the Philippines, wrote the following words in one of the approbations prefixed to Father Losa's work:—" Though I loved Gregory exceedingly, I did not often converse with or visit him, because he, not speaking unless questioned, and I bearing the title of Master—though, alas! deficient in much that I might have learnt from him—my talk might have seemed to him impertinent, though from so holy a soul such a thing is not to be expected."

Again, though all discourse of God is very worthy of commendation, yet Gregory never spoke on His divine perfections, with the vast numbers of devout and religious persons who flocked to visit him, unless pointedly asked to do so. And when he did answer, his replies, though they were full of the profoundest wisdom, were expressed without exaggeration or emphasis, in the plainest possible style. Moreover, when he had given an answer, he did not, like some people, go on talking, but cut his words short, when he had satisfied the demand made upon him. It often happened that the answer he gave raised many objections. All these he solved, when they were put to him, with the greatest brevity of words, but never volunteered to do so of his own accord, since he deemed such a proceeding unnecessary.

All this will appear the more virtuous, when we reflect what an itching men have to display the little knowledge they may possess. Yet here was a man who, we may say, knew the whole Bible by heart, who was an expert ascetical theologian, a skilful moralist, a deeply read historian, and blessed with so happy a memory that he could, at will, draw from his treasures things both old and new, nevertheless putting a guard upon his mouth, and a door of prudence upon his lips, that he might not offend in word. Father Losa, quaintly enough, remarks that if Eliphaz, the friend of Job, had known Gregory, he would have changed his mind with regard to the possibility of withholding the utterance of a word conceived in the heart. "Conceptum sermonem," asks that severe Eastern, "retinere, quis poterit?" Who can withhold a word he hath conceived?

"Gregory Lopez could," says Father Losa, perhaps with a rueful experience of his taciturnity, and the sharpness with which he now and then corrected that itching to speak, which was probably one of the good Father's weaknesses. One day, shortly after he had come to live with Gregory at Santa Fé, and before he had yet conquered a little vanity in displaying his knowledge, he tells us of a slight correction he received from his holy friend. Gregory had been telling him of a certain Emperor, who, with the waywardness of a child, would eat nothing when at sea but fresh meat, and when on land would insist on having fish brought to him alive. "That," exclaimed the Father, "was Heliogabalus!" Gregory looked at him, and then said: "Since we condemned his acts, it was but fitting that we should have concealed his name."

On another occasion, Father Losa had taken up his position at the window of their little cottage, to watch the progress of a furious storm that was raging at the time. He stretched out his hand to feel the violence of the rain, and remarked to Gregory, that it rained very hard. Scarcely had the words passed his lips, when a blinding flash of lightning shot out from the dark bank of clouds over their heads, and at the same moment Father Losa felt a sharp twinge in his hand, as if some of the electric fluid had struck him. He drew it in hurriedly, and then began to complain to Gregory of the pain he felt. The good man did not commiserate him;

on the contrary, he said to him: "Serve you right; you have been punished for employing a useless word. I saw, as well as you did, that it rained hard!"

Once, after giving the Father great edification, by something which he had communicated to him, he was asked by him, with some degree of pardonable curiosity, why he had not told him of it before. Gregory said: "Because I do not speak what I know, but only what is necessary." And *à propos* of this guardianship of his tongue, he, on another occasion, told him, that for the space of two years he had never spoken, except to salute his kind host, whom he saw but once for a minute every day.

This care to say no more than was needed, extended also to what he wrote. He had made it a rule with himself, never to answer any letter, except charity required it; and even then he wrote simply what was needful to answer the questions which had been put to him. Many of his letters contained no more than five or six lines. As an instance of this brevity, take the reply which he sent to the Viceroy, written at the end of the letter which had been sent by the Viceroy to him: "I will do that which in this you commend to me." Many would set this down to rudeness, and say that he must have been an uncouth boor, and knew no better; but such was not the case. Gregory was a highly polished gentleman, and his laconic method, both of speaking and of writing, must be attributed to heavenly prudence, and a desire not to offend in word.

The only occasions when he spoke without being

asked were, when he deemed it necessary to do so in defence of God's honour, or of his neighbour's good name; when the truths of Sacred Scripture were impugned, or the faith of the Catholic Church called in question. But even this he never attempted to do, unless no other person present undertook to do it. And, again, when any one was assaulted by grievous temptations, or attacked by some malady, which made him irritable and inclined to murmur, it was wonderful to hear the flow of eloquent words which poured from Gregory's lips, as he endeavoured to make the poor sufferer acknowledge his error, and admit that under these tribulations, sent from God, there lay hidden the treasures of the divine wisdom and mercy.

He also spared not his words, when he undertook to explain certain expressions of Scripture, which heretics, through ignorance, misunderstood, and wrested, as St. Peter expresses it, to their own damnation. On such occasions, he did not merely cite a few texts to prove his point, but after stating the sense of the passage in question, he brought to bear upon his interpretation of it, other matter from the sacred text, which elucidated still more the meaning which he had attributed to the place under dispute. He then brought up authority after authority, clinching them all by reasons so cogent, so clear, so conclusive, that those who knew how sparing he was of words, stood amazed, as well at the logical power of the man, as at the unexpected flood of weighty words, that swept all disputatious cavilling before them, like chaff before the wind.

CHAPTER VI.

HIS WISDOM IN WORD AND WORK.

A VERY eminent man of the present century has said, that the next great power in the world, after that of speech, is the power of silence. We shall not, then, be very far wrong in saying, that if the number of really good talkers be small, the number of good listeners is equally so; and we may safely conclude, that a wise man is just as much known by his silence as by his words. If this be admitted as a criterion, it will speak very favourably of Gregory Lopez. He knew when to keep silence and when to speak,—what to say, and how to say it; and men judged of his wisdom, no less by the pertinent answers which he gave to pertinent questions, than by that wise discretion, which taught him when to seal up his lips at the right moment. Among those who came to visit him, there was a learned Doctor, who desired very much to have a discussion with him upon spiritual matters, and enlisted Father Losa on his side, earnestly beseeching him to draw his friend out, and make him discourse upon certain points which he suggested. The good man was so eager, that he did not wait for his ally to open the attack, but began it himself. He did this, by putting a multitude of objections and questions to him upon the matters which he wished to know.

He flung them at his head, so to speak, and hardly gave him time to put in a word, before he started off on a fresh theme. Judged by the standard of wisdom given by most philosophers, this individual would hardly have merited his title of Doctor; and perhaps Gregory would have been on their side. Whatever his opinion was, he kept it to himself. Father Losa, anxious, no doubt, that Gregory should make a favourable impression upon the visitor, made signs to him to answer the objections urged against the thesis proposed. But Gregory was not to be moved. The good Doctor, it appears, was deaf, and Gregory whispered, in a voice sufficiently audible to reach the ear of the Father without being intelligible to his guest: "He is more edified by silence than by speaking," and answered not a word. Though the Doctor was under his roof for two whole days, he received not a single syllable in answer to his ceaseless flow of words. Father Losa, wondering what impression had been made upon their loquacious guest by this proceeding, asked him as he was leaving, what he thought of Gregory. It turned out as Gregory had said: his silence had been most pleasing to him. His estimate of the holy man was partial, no doubt; for most great talkers are fond of the sound of their own voice, and are delighted to meet with that rarity in the present age,—a good, intelligent listener. With respect to this same interview, Gregory himself afterwards made this remark: "I see many, my dear Father, who talk well; let us *do* well."

If any one, to test his knowledge of those languages

of which he naturally knew nothing, put questions to him in Latin, he would say, with great calmness: "What is that in Spanish?" and, being told, he would answer: "The matter is as you say." He thus intimated that no answer was needed. He also frequently asked the learned, the meaning of some Latin text, as if he himself knew nothing of it, thus humbling himself in their presence.

His prudence in answering people who consulted him about their worldly affairs was admirable. It would be well for us to imitate his reserve, for many involve themselves in endless difficulties, by being over-eager to mix themselves up with that which in no way concerns them. Thus, when asked by some disappointed colonist whether he ought to return to Spain, or by a young couple whether they ought to marry, his invariable answer was: "I will commend it to God, because, in affairs of this nature, it is proper that God should dispose the means and move the wills of the parties concerned, to do what will conduce most to His glory, and to the good of society at large."

But when any persons came to consult him about their vocation to the religious, or the ecclesiastical state, he first of all discovered whether they possessed the qualifications requisite for those high callings. If he saw that they were endowed with these, he did all in his power to urge them to follow after, and embrace the greater good. If, however, he perceived them to be wanting in these requisites, his usual answer was: "I will commend the matter to God." He was a great defender and lover of Religious Orders, and ever spoke of them with the highest esteem, we might almost say veneration. It seemed to be a fixed idea of his, a kind of a duty incumbent upon him, to take every opportunity of showing secular persons, how pre-eminently superior the religious state was to theirs, how full it was of the Spirit of God, how, in a word, Religious were God's chosen band, and His picked soldiers. With reference to the security to be found in Communities, he used to say : " A tree that stands alone upon the plain, assailed by all the winds of heaven, had need strike its roots downwards, and take a firm hold in the soil ; but one that stands in the forest is secure from every blast." Like a profoundly sensible man, he was very loth to pass judgment upon those in authority. He knew full well, how easy a thing it is for a subject to be mistaken, in viewing the acts of Superiors, because his field of vision is so limited ; and had he not been a highly spiritual man, he would have looked with contemptuous pity upon those who pompously criticise the acts of kings, and governors, and generals, and most frequently their own immediate Superiors, as if they could have done much better themselves. Though he very mildly reproved such as ventured to speak disparagingly of them in his presence, still, the rebuke, coming from him, no matter how gently administered, was felt more than the most stinging remark from another. He usually said to such : " If you were in their place, you would not do so well. Who has set us up to meddle with governments ? You should tell this to those who are in authority, for of what use is it talking to us here?" Gregory, as a matter of course, met with that numerous class of spiritual shams, who, professing to be religious, give themselves free licence to say things to the detriment of others, which ordinary Christians look upon as grievous sins. He held the same view about such charlatans as the Apostle St. James. "I do not," he used to say, "account him a spiritual, no, nor even a virtuous man, who judges, or speaks ill of another." His usual method of extinguishing these was by saying, in his quiet, unimpassioned way: "What you speak of can't be remedied here; let us say no more about it."

In fact Gregory would never say behind a man's back, what he was afraid to tell him to his face. If we were all to imitate him in this respect, the vice of detraction would speedily disappear from the world.

His wisdom was also manifested, by the dexterity he displayed in conversing with the various classes of men with whom he came in contact. He was at home with them all, and managed the conversation with such admirable skill, that he never led them into subjects which were beyond their capacity. With the husbandman, he conversed with as much ease as with the lawyer; and the soldier found in him, one, who while treating with him of marches, and battles, and ambuscades, was putting into his heart from these matters, maxims of eternal wisdom, bearing fruit unto everlasting life. With those whose lives were given up to spirituality, he loved most of all to converse. But, as it not unfrequently happens that some of these are led to the kingdom of God by one course of spiritual exercises, and some by another, such as have not that breadth of mind which enables men to see in the diversity of spirits, the working of the same God, occasionally began to censure those who did not exactly do as they did. Gregory knowing this tendency of poor weak human nature, always anticipated and prevented such tirades, by expressing the pleasure it gave him to contemplate the great variety of spirits existing in the Church of God. This diversity, he maintained, was one of the beauties of the heavenly Jerusalem. On this particular point he used to reason somewhat after this fashion. "In all spiritual matters, God is the master. No one, therefore, ought to constitute himself master of another, either to judge him, or to lead him in the way in which he himself is led by God; for, if with God there is a variety of ways, then each of them is good, and those who are conducted in them are right in pursuing their course, and ought not to be disturbed."

To such as asked him what they ought to do to gain eternal life, he gave substantially the same answer as our Lord did to those who put to Him a similar question; "Love God," he would say, "and your neighbour! That is the royal and perfect way for all, from the least to the greatest. There can be no deceit in it, for it is our law in which consists all perfection."

Another of his sayings was:—"To be always talking of the Spirit and of spiritual things, betrays a milk-and-watery disposition. It is a temptation to which novices are subject." And again:—Though a man possessed the intellectual power of a Seraph, he should not desire to make this known without necessity.

He considered it far better to recommend one's neighbour to God, than to talk to him of God, unless indeed some particular necessity required it, and hence he used frequently to say: "It is better to speak *with* God than *of* God."

To a man who thought himself spiritual, but yet felt no desire to be rid of this present life, he said: "It would be a cause of shame to you if this were known of you; for since St. Paul says: 'We have not here a lasting city, but seek one that is to come,' he cannot be a truly spiritual man who does not long for that spiritual state."

When he heard of any great or miraculous occurrences, his usual expression was: "One grain of God's pure love is worth more than all this noise." He was once asked by a certain gentleman, whether perfect men indulged in any little sensible gratifications. "Yes," he replied, "for when a man is on a journey, he loves to see his horse eat"—for so he termed his body,—"but," he added, "one that is perfect keeps a tight rein on his body in such matters, whereas the imperfect take no care to do so, but at one time immoderately torment their spirit, while at another they allow it to be carried away by every wind that blows."

Whenever any one, either in conversation or in action, was guilty of some solecism, or awkwardness, which made him ridiculous and raised a laugh at his expense, Gregory took special care not even to smile, but by his compassionate looks testified how he felt for, and condoled with the unlucky individual. So also when persons afflicted with any infirmity presented themselves before him, he manifested such genuine compassion for their misfortunes as not unfrequently to send them away full of consolation.

This was especially noticed in the case of a lady of high rank, who came to Santa Fé in great grief and could not be comforted. All the efforts of Father Losa to assuage her sorrow, were ineffectual. A few words from Gregory, however, had such a magical effect upon her, that she went away with a light heart and smiling countenance, saying: "I am perfectly satisfied."

People who visited him, frequently discussed in his presence, matters which were involved in great obscurity, and concerning which the authorities for and against were very evenly balanced. After long and warm debates, during which Gregory usually played the part of the listener, the matter would be occasionally referred to him. His ordinary answer on such occasions was: "The morning will come, and we shall be wiser." By this he implied, that to solve doubts of that nature required time, that they might be laid before God. He did not wish it to be understood from this that he would ask light of God, and so be enabled to answer the difficulty. His humility was too great to presume so much. Many looked upon this answer of his, as having reference to the time of death, for then indeed all our difficulties will be cleared up.

He very prudently repressed all external manifestations of devotion, lest men should think more highly of him than he deserved. Hence one could see in him when hearing Mass, receiving Holy Communion, or performing any other act of piety, nothing extraordinary, except indeed it were his great recollection which filled all beholders with admiration.

Another practice of his might be recommended with advantage to many devout people of the present age, and that is, the strictness with which he observed silence in church. While there, he would never engage in any conversation, or even open his lips to speak a few words. If by any chance he deemed it necessary to speak, he used to leave the church, and transact the business outside. Let those who are not ashamed to hold conversations in the holy place, to nod, and smile, and wave their hands in recognition of friends, remember this, and when tempted to behave in so unbecoming a manner, awaken their faith, ask themselves, Who is there present? and then imitate Gregory.

CHAPTER VII.

HIS COURAGE AND MAGNANIMITY.

TO the generality of mankind, it will doubtless seem paradoxical to say, that to be a Saint, requires as much courage, determination, and magnanimity, as is necessary to form one of those characters which the popular voice would call heroical. We say that such a statement as this would seem paradoxical; for men, as a rule, look upon the absence of those qualities which go to make up the popular idea of a hero, as the very groundwork on which sanctity is built. This widely-spread opinion can only be dissipated by deep and serious thought. Its existence amongst us indicates a certain baseness in our nature, which is prone to regard that only as really great which is carnal, and enables men, by brute force, to conquer and prevail over their fellows. But any one who attentively considers the matter, will discover that this is false. If he take the trouble to examine the life of one of God's Saints, he will see that the Saint has all the qualities which the popular hero possesses, without any of his vices, and many others beside, to which the hero can lay no claim. He will also probably discover, that whereas the Saint is always a hero, the hero is not always a Saint.

We say, then, that Gregory Lopez, during his life, displayed as much, if not far more, true courage and magnanimity than many of those to whom the title of hero has been given, and to whom statues have been erected by their admiring fellow-men; because the only claim of such heroes to this proud distinction, has not unfrequently been the possession of that courage, which is not, by any means, uncommon in many orders of the brute creation. The courage, however, displayed by Gregory is of a far higher order, and argues a loftiness of soul which all will admire, but few attempt to emulate. In him we behold a man, still in the flower of his youth, fair to look upon, rich in mental qualities, the scion, most probably, of a noble house, with every chance of bearing off victoriously the most glittering prizes in the race of life, and yet deliberately turning his back upon the glorious prospect, and choosing instead, to leave home and fatherland, to go into exile, and live among a savage people, hostile to his Religion and to his race.

When we reflect upon the nature of that life, we can easily understand why so few "go and do in like manner." They are content, indeed, to admire, but do not imitate, because mere natural heroism is not equal to the task; for although to be a hero, even of this kind, demands a certain amount of self-sacrifice, yet it does not require that total elimination of self, without which a life such as Gregory led is an impossibility. Let any one who wishes clearly to understand this, examine the matter for himself. Take, for instance, his union with God. To keep that union unbroken, as he kept it, was an act of more than human courage. In order to effect this, he never said or did anything, which was not conformable to the Divine Will. He so managed his interior powers, as to make everything that could interrupt it, cease; and to allow no image to remain in his memory, which might disturb it for the shortest space of time. Of course we must admit, that this power came from God, from Whom is every good and perfect gift. But this will not lessen our esteem for the courage which made him adhere to the Helper, by Whose aid he persevered for so many years in that strait way, with such profound recollection and silence, in the midst of innumerable inconveniences, and poverty the most complete that it is possible to conceive.

The nature of his heroism will perhaps be brought into still clearer light, if we glance at the enemies he had to encounter, the conflicts he had to endure, and the field in which those conflicts had to be fought.

Like the most part of ordinary Christians, he had to encounter those enemies which each man must overcome or be thrust by them into the fire of hell. The great difference between his conflict and theirs was, that the rage of the devil burnt more fiercely against him than against the common run of devout men. In the persons of such as Gregory, the devil, so to speak, "meets foemen worthy of his steel," and to compass their destruction, he puts forth all the power, the subtlety, and the malignity of his perverted nature.

Hence we find him assaulting Gregory with the most frightful temptations, and causing him to be molested by sinful men, who, seeing that his works were contrary to theirs, and cast a kind of reproach upon them, attacked him with the keen weapon of the tongue, and raised up against him false reports and unworthy suspicions. All these eventually proved to be groundless and redounded to his honour, instead of covering him with confusion.

But if it be a great trial to be persecuted by the wicked, how much more bitter and unendurable must it have been for Gregory, when good men—upright, honest, and religious men—by God's permission, rose against him, and, mistaking his motives and the whole tenor of his life, began to attack and vilify him? Added to this, there was that continual trial which a man suffers from himself,—the Flesh dragging him in one direction, the Spirit in another directly opposite. At times also God Himself seemed to abandon him and leave him to himself, to bear up the weight of his many infirmities, unaided either by heaven or by earth. The lamp of God no longer shone over his head, nor did God dwell secretly with him in his tabernacle, but was apparently deaf to his prayer, and granted not his petitions.

Moreover, there were conflicts innumerable to be engaged in with those unseen foes "whose name is legion." He who knows what those enemies are, will readily understand with what subtle skill they manage their attacks, and with what untiring zeal they return again and again when repulsed, ever finding an ally in corrupt nature, ready to league with them in compassing his destruction.

A circumstance in this warfare which adds not a little to the glory of him who proves himself a good soldier therein, and which serves to bring out into clearer light his courage and his powers of endurance, is the ground whereon this bitter conflict must be fought. This is no other than a man's interior, where the Spirit wars against the Flesh and the Flesh against the Spirit. The pain caused by this domestic conflict is very great. He who gives, and he who takes the blows is made equally to smart; and the victory over the Flesh is won only by extraordinary and untiring vigilance. This is but natural, since, to the innate strength of the Flesh—which, in our present state, is a match for the unaided Spirit—there is joined the power of the devil, who, with a skill peculiarly his own, guides the forces leagued against the soul, with all the dexterity of an able and experienced tactician.

Taking into consideration, then, the anguish Gregory endured in the course of this interior conflict, and the virtues which, notwithstanding the turmoil of that conflict, he cultivated in his heart, some idea may be formed of his courage and indomitable perseverance; especially if we reflect upon certain circumstances, which, of their own nature, were calculated to dissipate the one and break through the other. In the first place, his heart was so full of charity towards his neighbour, that, like the great Apostle, " he wept with those that wept," and thus shared all their tribulations and calamities; but, " while rejoicing with those that rejoiced," he did not, on the other hand, partake of their joy. By an heroic act of the will, he had shut off all that from himself, being quite content to bear the burthens of others without anything to alleviate their weight. In the second place, to use the quaint phrase of his biographer : " He eat the bread of sorrow every day very dry." He had none of that sensible spiritual sweetness, which God oftentimes gives to His servants, to sustain and comfort them in the midst of their secret trials. Like a brave soldier, who casts aside and makes little of the creature comforts which punier men covet, and seek after with so much eagerness, Gregory was so far from desiring these favours from God, that he actually prayed Him to withhold them from him, because he was willing to serve Him for His own sake alone. Hence, with this view, he had prayed God to withdraw from him the gift of tears, with which he had been favoured in the beginning of his conversion. Again, though burning with the desire to see the Sacred Humanity of Christ, he begged of God to mitigate it, because he found that he was thereby held back and his resignation to the Divine Will somewhat diminished. In fact, he rejected all those consolations which the devout servants of God experience from time to time, preferring to serve Him without pay in this world, and feeling a holy joy that He was leading him to Himself by the sure, safe, but painful way of His Holy Cross. Hence we find him, when looked upon as a heretic, or a fool, or an idle vagabond, never excusing or defending himself, but rather defending and justifying those who spoke against him.

The means he took for preserving in his soul a peace, so profound that it could not be ruffled by any words of slander, or storm of contumely, will be best learned from an answer he once gave to an officious friend, who spoke to him of the great feelings of hostility which certain individuals bore against him : " God forbid," said he, " that I should dissipate or distract my mind by thinking of the like."

Another answer of his, slightly tinged with playful sarcasm, shows how little account he made of what others thought about him. It will perhaps incite us to imitate him, and thus make us less painfully alive to those barbed shafts of uncharitableness, which certain natures delight to launch against their neighbours. A nobleman of some distinction was, it appears, once making inquiries into the state of the Hospital at Guasteca. These were addressed to Father Losa, who, after satisfying him on all points, could not resist the temptation, to speak to him about Gregory, whom he looked upon as his spiritual father and friend. The nobleman does not, however, seem to have been in any way impressed by the glowing account he received of Gregory's solitude, and holy spirit. He was one of those shrewd, practical men, who seem incapable of any emotion, save that engendered by adding up figures, comparing totals, and examining results. The first question he asked was, " What business has a man of that character to be in the Hospital ? What plea can he urge, to justify his stay in a place destined for the sick ? I tell you what I would do with all such as he; they should all receive at my hands two hundred lashes apiece." Father Losa was rather taken aback by this view of Gregory's life, and as a matter of course, took care to inform his friend of what had been said about him. Gregory was rather amused by the sentiments of this Philistine towards him, and with his usual placid smile said : " Well, he is pretty right after all; for an idle fellow like myself, richly deserves two hundred stripes. However, noblemen full of worldly business can hardly conceive what internal exercises are."

Though the visits of persons of high rank were by no means unfrequent to his humble abode, they were not by any means received by him with pleasure. Like all the Saints, he shrank from publicity and from being in the minds and mouths of men, with as much eagerness as worldlings display in courting notoriety. Frequent, in consequence, were the chidings he administered to Father Losa for his officious loquacity. This good man was never tired of trumpeting Gregory's praise, much to his annoyance and confusion, who, if anything, rather disliked the visits of Prelates, Viceroys, and Noblemen, and when occasion served, showed with all gravity and humility, that they were rather a source of trouble, than of honour to him. For although he had a very high esteem for the prudence and piety of the Viceroy, Duke Louis de Velasco, he nevertheless wrote to him, and requested him to forbear his visits, alleging reasons to him for this, which completely satisfied him, and made him forego one of the greatest pleasures he had—a few minutes' conference with so holy a servant of God. Gregory's indifference to human praise or blame was manifestly shown when his writings on the Apocalypse began to be known and talked of. They were looked upon by the most competent critics, as works of great merit, and the reputation they gained for their author, made him known far and wide among the people. Whenever mention was made of this performance in his presence, he listened as if the commendation were given to the work of another man. An opportunity of testing his equanimity under the sting of censure, was very soon afforded him ; for the Inquisition, with that watchful care, by which it seeks to guard the faithful from false doctrine, ordered the book to be examined. The mere fact of such an order, emanating from such a source, seemed for the moment to cast a doubt upon his orthodoxy, or at least to indicate, that there was a suspicion of his incapacity to comment on a book of such deep mystery, without being guilty of gross errors. Yet not a sign or a word escaped his lips, which could give the slightest indication whereby men could judge, if he were in any way troubled by the order. This trial, if trial it can be called, turned out to his greater glory; for the book being given to Don Pedro de Agurto for examination, that prelate after a careful study of its doctrine, declared that it was perfectly sound and orthodox. "I have never," said he, "seen a better exposition of those divine revelations. I wonder that so much can be said so convincingly, and yet so briefly. The knowledge of history evinced in these pages, is greater than I ever remember to have met with, in any other writer. It is not, therefore, too much to say, that I believe he had the assistance of the Holy Spirit to aid him in the composition of that book."

His dislike of publicity, caused him to conceal with wonderful fortitude any pain he suffered, lest people should gather round to compassionate him, and then talk of his patience and virtue. He was not, however, unwilling at times, to relate, for the good of others, what had befallen him in times past; and thus a knowledge of much of his interior life has been preserved for our edification. At various times throughout the year he used to be seized with most painful attacks of colic, which, though causing him exquisite torture, never wrung from his lips a groan or a word of complaint, nor altered the sweet serenity of his features, nor the ordinary posture of his body. The only indication of his sufferings, appeared in the extreme weakness which seized upon him after these attacks, and in the worn look of his pallid face. Father Losa thus used to learn when he was, or had been unwell. He once asked him, when he was in this condition, what it was that had brought him so low, and Gregory replied: "I have had the colic for the last fifteen days without a moment's respite." He was very subject to a species of intermittent fever. The remedy he used for conquering this, was a rigid abstinence,—which lasted usually for five days together,—from every species of food. And yet, though subject to these infirmities, he never succumbed to his malady, as ordinary men would have done, and retired to bed for repose; but continued to go about and perform his ordinary exercises, as if he were in perfect health.

During his residence at Santa Fé, he had the toothache for a year, with scarcely an hour's relief from pain during the whole of that time. This was discovered by his gathering and applying to his face, certain herbs, with whose healing properties he was well acquainted, and occasionally also by his inability to eat anything. When he was obliged to part with one of his teeth which gave him great pain, he would not suffer the operation to be performed by the dentist, but did it himself in a way which occasioned him more torture. All these instances serve to show us his love of suffering, and to point him out to us, as a man so dead to all self-gratification, that he sought pain with as much eagerness, as men of the world run after pleasure.

He once told Father Losa that the devil had, on one occasion, come to tempt him under a visible form. "In what way," asked the Father, "did you defend yourself?" "I thought," answered Gregory, "that I could do nothing better to vanquish him, than what I then happened to be doing, so I continued it with all my power. Thereupon the devil vanished, and never afterwards tempted me visibly."

Gregory was never heard to utter any maxim, or to give any good advice, which he did not himself put in practice in time of need. Among his many wise sayings, the following was frequently in his mouth:— "Misery is not to be desired; but the bearing of it with patience, when it comes upon us, is exceedingly to be sought for." When, therefore, anguish of soul or body seized upon him, he bore it with as much evenness of mind, as if he were a man, not of flesh and blood, but of adamant. This power of patient endurance threw around him a certain air of loftiness and majesty, which is rarely to be met with in men. It was a thing which struck one after a short acquaintance with him; nor did familiar intercourse, as is too often the case, destroy this impression.

As, then, we judge of a man's courage, perseverance, energy, and talent by the height to which he raises himself by his own unaided exertions; and consider him to have been possessed of all these qualities, who, for example, exalts himself from the rank of a common soldier, to wield the Field-Marshal's baton, so we may be led to infer similar qualities of mind in him, who, being a poor, abject son of Adam, becomes a Saint in the Church of God.

Having, then, ample proof in the life of Gregory, that by the help of God's grace, he was enabled to ascend into those heights of sanctity, unto which it is not given for every man to aspire, it is fitting that we should do our utmost to make known that sanctity which he so studiously tried to conceal, in order that "God may be glorified in His Saints." The reason he so carefully kept his high sanctity from the eyes of men, was revealed one day by him to Father Losa, who had taken him rather sharply to task for his closeness. "To conceal virtue," said Gregory, "is no difficulty for one who has a lively faith. For, if a man firmly believe that all his virtues shall be seen in the kingdom of heaven, what need he care for their not being known in the village of this world?"

CHAPTER VIII.

HIS HUMILITY AND INTERIOR POVERTY.

TO be internally poor, is to have arrived at that state of christian perfection, upon which our Lord pronounced a blessing: "Blessed are the poor in spirit; for theirs is the kingdom of heaven." It consists in stripping the heart of all affection to created things, in order that it may have no hindrance, no clog, to prevent it from flying upwards to union with God. To speak worthily of this virtue, one must practise it. The mere study of it, will not aid one to do it that justice which it deserves. All, then, that we can do, is to narrate those few indications of it, which fell under the observation of Father Losa, and the hints of its existence, gathered from what he heard, in the various answers which Gregory gave to different persons.

The first object upon which a man fastens his affections, and the last from which he can succeed in loosing them, is himself. There is a passionate fondness in this love of self, which causes it to strike its roots down so deeply, and to lay hold of its object with such a tenacious grasp, that the difficulty of dislodging it from the heart, where it has once established its tyranny, is easily accounted for. There is no room there for anything else: all else must yield it place; all else must bow down and do it homage. There is nothing so high, nothing so excellent, nothing so holy, as that idol, self. This is to be rich in spirit, to abound in pride. From this species of riches Gregory was most free. He had divested himself of them, and cast them out of his heart. Self was to him the last personage in the world, and, being a just, a rigorously just man, he gave to it all the consideration which it deserved. With him, consequently, self was ever put after all others, and in the lowest place. He was frequently heard to say: " Since I betook myself to solitude, I never judged any man. I account all better, and wiser than myself; and, consequently, except when asked, I have never counselled, nor made myself a master to any one." Those who lived with him could bear witness to the truth of these words, and also to the fact, that God made him a master and a guide to many, perhaps because he did not thrust himself forward to be either the one or the other; "for those who thus humble themselves, shall be exalted." What a boon it would be to society at large, if those who have neither the virtue, nor the mental qualifications to teach and guide their fellow-men, would be content to remain in obscurity, and not seek to climb into positions for which they are utterly unsuited, and whence they will most assuredly fall, covered, it may be, with eternal confusion. "He that exalteth himself shall be humbled." Being full of that poverty of spirit, or humility, which is the same thing, he was most careful to excuse all those who in any way differed from him, or blamed him. In the course of this short history, we have frequently had to mention the officiousness of those who were his friends, and kept him *au courant* with the tittle-tattle which was going about concerning him. Here, again, we are forced to record another instance of this mistaken kindness, in order to show Gregory's humility. A certain person one day told him, with questionable propriety, that there were many, who seriously detracted him. To this Gregory made answer: "I have always excused them, not in words only, but with all my heart, in deed and in truth."

His poverty of spirit led him also never to premeditate what he might be called upon to say upon any subject. If he ever had the slightest ambition to have his sayings chronicled, and passed from mouth to mouth as things of some worth, it was entirely extinguished by a little incident which befell him, shortly before he began his solitary life. It appears that some question was submitted to him for explanation, upon which he expended much time and thought in selecting various reasons to support the view he took of the matter. No opportunity, however, occurred for putting them forward, and from this circumstance he learnt a lesson. He saw that it was vain and profitless to waste time in composing set discourses, for which there might, probably, never be any use. Ever after this he relied upon God to furnish him both with words and matter, for everything he might have to say. This trust in his good Father was not misplaced, for the Lord filled his heart with divine wisdom, and out of the abundance of that treasure-house he drew as occasion demanded, whatever he deemed conducive to the edification of his neighbour. He was a living example of God's choice of the humble, to be the recipients of those treasures of wisdom, which are so studiously withheld from the self-sufficient and pretentious pedants of this world.

The very idea that he might be thought wiser, or better than the most ordinary Christian, caused him much pain. One may easily conjecture, then, what his suffering was when his extraordinary sanctity, or the divine favours bestowed upon him, were hinted at in his presence. This was shown in a very marked manner, little more than a week before his death. A very intimate friend, a holy and religious man, came to visit him, and seeing how ill he was, thought it his duty to let him know, how very near he was to the supreme and awful moment of death. For this purpose, he said in a familiar way: "Well, I suppose you are going to enjoy our Blessed Lord!" Gregory, imagining that his friend believed him to have been divinely forewarned of his approaching dissolution, answered with some degree of astonishment: "How can your Reverence believe that I know the hour of my death? I do not deserve such a favour."

This low estimation of himself, shone forth still more clearly a few days before his death, while he was lying helplessly upon his bed of pain. An Indian woman came to visit him, and as she spoke with Father Losa in her own language, which was unintelligible to Gregory, he said to the Father: "Mark well what she says, for probably her advice will be advantageous to me." Thus did he place himself beneath all, even the most lowly, and imagine that their counsel would profit him at the close of his life, and teach him how to die well.

He was also entirely free from that forecasting of the future, in which proud men so frequently busy themselves. For they whose hearts are cankered with pride, are ever imagining what will befall them some years hence; whether they shall obtain possession of that dignity after which they are aspiring; whether they shall become famous; whether their fortune will be augmented, and the like. Now Gregory, mindful of Christ's words, "Sufficient for the day is the evil thereof," completely shut out that future from all his calculations, leaving it entirely in the hands of God, and trusting himself to

His keeping, to receive whatsoever it should please his Heavenly Father to send. He had no aspiration to fill a higher station than that in which he found himself. He repeated continually to himself: "I am nothing; I am good for nothing." In consequence of his trust in God's Providence, and his idea of his own nothingness, he would not suffer any one to make any provision for him for the future. Father Losa, therefore, had to be circumspect when seeking for a more healthy situation for him to live in; for when Gregory had any suspicion that he was taking any steps to see to his future wellbeing, he would frequently say to him: "Let no one be troubled for me; God will take care to provide what is best pleasing to His Divine Majesty."

Curiosity was another thing of which he carefully emptied his heart. It is an imperfection from which many holy persons cannot rid themselves, without great difficulty. But Gregory, having once embraced his solitary mode of life, never desired to see anything in the world. There was no hankering in his heart to see friends, or country, or kindred. He was also perfectly free from that curiosity which the holiest souls not unfrequently feel, to see Angels, to have ecstasies, and to receive revelations from God.

His only desire was to see God. It was a desire full of the deepest resignation. "God," he used to say, "will reveal Himself to me, when it shall please, and how it shall please His Divine Majesty. The only ecstasy he longed for, was to be united to God, and to become every day more conformed to His holy Will.

It is easy to conceive, how a soul full of such dispositions, would never seek its joy in any earthly object, nor admit into the heart any pleasure whose source was of this world. His chief delight was God, and in that pleasure, which springs from the fact of working for Him, and for the good of his neighbour. Father Losa looked upon this, as virtue of a very high order, and ventured to tell Gregory as much, but he was rather surprised to find he did not esteem it to be of so exalted a nature. "It is a shame for us who live under the law of Grace," said he, "to look upon that, as the sublimest virtue, to which one living under the law of fear could attain, though surrounded by everything calculated to render its attainment most difficult. For we read of Esther, the wife of a great Monarch, the first in a brilliant Court, that she testified to the Lord and said: 'Thou knowest well, my God and my Lord, that since I was brought to this palace till this present day, Thy handmaid hath not rejoiced, save only in Thee.' A proof of this alienation of his heart from all earthly joy, is furnished by the manner in which he ever treated Father Losa. This good Father, from the first moment he saw Gregory at our Lady of Remedies, had conceived for him a very strong affection; in fact it was so strong, that he would willingly have become his slave. Nor did this prove, as so many sudden affections do, of very short duration. It continued with unabated fervour from the moment he first set eyes upon him, till eighteen years after, when Gregory breathed forth his soul in his arms. An affection so deep, so lasting, and proved by so many deeds, could not, and did not escape the notice of the holy man, who, at times, chided him for it; yet, though conscious of the love and veneration in which he was held by Father Losa, he never relied upon it, nor put the least trust in what he did, or could do for him. This was the result of no insensibility, but arose from the vivid manner in which he saw God as the Author of all the good done him, and the creature simply as the instrument employed by that best of Fathers to convey His benefits to His children. Hence his gratitude to benefactors was given to God, Whom he prayed, with all his heart, to shower down blessings upon them in return for the good, which He had moved their hearts to do unto him. This was a fixed idea with him, and the sole aim he had in every act, whereby he sought to benefit others. Hence in all that he did for them, he strove to make those, whom he benefited, return thanks, and feel love,—not for himself, since he was but an instrument,—but for God, Who is the chief worker of all the good that flows upon man.

CHAPTER IX.

HIS EXTERNAL POVERTY.

TO be poor in spirit, is without doubt, a great virtue; for He, Who through love of us became poor, has declared, that all such are truly blessed. Nevertheless, to be simply detached from all earthly possessions, is not the highest degree of the virtue of poverty. It argues a higher degree still, when to this detachment there is superadded the voluntary renunciation of all power to possess, or hold dominion over the goods of this world. We therefore find Gregory, who ever aspired after what was most perfect, divesting himself of the right to call anything his own, as soon as he had taken the all-important step of entering upon a solitary life. He regarded those who, like himself, were stripped both in affection and in reality of all worldly goods, as the only men who could truly be called rich. Hence his love for that state in which Christ lived during his mortal life, made him ingenious in discovering ways by which to make his own life resemble it as nearly as possible. Thus, he never adhered to any determined fashion in his dress, nor in the material out of which it was made, but wore whatever God sent him. For the first eleven years of his solitary life, it was composed of coarse sackcloth, but when he was living at Atrisco, the charitable gentleman who entertained him, gave him some grey cloth, and out of this he made his clothes. No costlier material was ever used by him during the rest of his life.

In his first years of solitude, and in fact as long as his strength was unimpaired, he had no other bed whereon to rest his weary limbs, than the bare earth. After some time, when he began to be infirm, he lay upon a few sheepskins stretched upon the ground. As his bodily weakness and ailments increased, there was added to these a sort of thin mattress; Father Losa calls it a quilt, and then a thin coverlet to throw over him as he lay asleep. Nothing could exceed the poverty of the little room in which he lived. It was absolutely unadorned, nor would he suffer any one to hide the bare walls, by putting up curtains, even of the coarsest material. He washed his own clothes, and was ever remarkable for cleanliness, and the good Father observes, doubtless with some surprise, that he washed his feet at times, and would not suffer another to do this for him. This may have been extraordinary in a Spaniard at that time, and in a country where slaves to do such menial offices were in abundance; but to our notions it was only proper and a matter of course. Another reason for mentioning this fact so particularly, may have been to give an idea of his virginal modesty, for he remarks, that no one ever saw his naked flesh.

His diet was most frugal, and his temperance and mortification in what he eat so great, that no illness ever happened to him through self-indulgence. This is a thing which cannot be said, even by those who are, ordinarily speaking, very abstemious; for they are at times tempted to go beyond the bounds they have set for themselves, and suffer in consequence. To avoid sickness resulting from this cause was a strong motive, though not the strongest, which urged Gregory to this severe treatment of himself; for being a poor man, he said that all such as he, ought to be very careful for their health, that they might not fall sick and become a burthen to others. In the little that he did eat, he rarely, if ever, allowed flesh meat to form a part of his meal, but rigorously abstained from partaking of it as long as

11

he led a strictly retired life. When, however, he began to mix a little with other people, he relaxed this rule somewhat, and eat whatever was set before him. He scarcely ever eat more than once a day. His sole earthly possessions were a globe and map which he had made, as we have already observed, with his own hands. Also two books, written by himself.

It would seem as if Almighty God designed Gregory to be unto men, a living example of His own tender loving providence; for by the inspiration of the Holy Spirit, under Whose guidance Gregory ordered his life, he learnt, that it was God's Will he should never ask for anything, but depend entirely upon the loving and watchful care of his Lord. Hence he never by word or sign solicited any one to bestow an alms upon him. If God at times allowed him to suffer great inconvenience on this account, it was not through any want of care on His part, but in order to increase the glory of His faithful servant in heaven. The trials which he had to endure in consequence, were occasionally very hard to bear, because oftentimes, in the course of his travels, he came weary, footsore, and hungry to some place of refreshment, and as he asked for nothing, nothing was given to him. Hence, he not unfrequently had to lie upon the hard ground, and rise in the morning to pursue his journey, without having tasted a morsel of food. Thus did he encounter hunger, thirst, labour, and weariness for the love of God. One would be inclined to think, that seeing his condition, charitable people would have supplied his wants. But Father Losa remarks, that men were deterred from offering Gregory an alms, because he was so far from having the appearance of one in need, that on the contrary, he looked more like a lord, or a man in affluent circumstances, than one who in reality was poorer than the poorest mendicant. The loving eye of his friend Father Losa quickly detected the great pain which this determination, not to ask for anything, was continually causing Gregory, and he one day said to him: "For my part, I think that if I stood in need of anything, I would ask for it, in order to humble myself." He answered: "I would not." Father Losa urged, that it would be doing amiss, not to ask for what was necessary. Gregory replied: "For you it might be so, but not for me; because God conducts each one in His own particular way." As an instance of the manner in which he carried out this principle, which, under the guidance of God, he had established for himself, we may state, that his increasing infirmities had rendered it necessary for him in his latter years to take every morning a draught of wine. If he omitted to do so, he was tormented with a most racking colic. Being fully aware of his principles, the good Father was also very careful to provide him with this little comfort. But in spite of his most watchful care, Gregory had, occasionally, to do without his medicine, and resign himself to the agonies he suffered; for though the wine was given him regularly enough, there were times when the little stock was exhausted, and his good friend did not become aware of it till it was too late to procure more. Father Losa found this out, more than once, by the paleness of

Gregory's face, and by the weary, exhausted drooping of his emaciated frame. On one of these occasions he asked what was the cause of this debility, and Gregory answered: "For several days I have not had my draught of wine, and have consequently been in great pain." The Father was very much troubled at this, because he happened not to have any in the house; but God came to his assistance, in a wonderful manner; for just at that moment a friend of his arrived, bringing with him a little of the very best wine the country could produce.

Gregory carried out his principle, of not asking for anything, even in the smallest matters. For instance: Father Losa one day found him making thread out of a piece of linen. Knowing that Gregory must have been aware, that there was no lack of it in the house, he asked him what that was for. "To sew with," answered Gregory; and it then appeared that his clothes wanted mending, but that no thread had been given him for the purpose. Father Losa, seeing that God was leading him by the way of perfect reliance upon His Providence, conceived the notion that it might be part of the Divine plan that he himself should supply the servant of God with all that he needed. He submitted this to Gregory's judgment, who no doubt concurred in the view of the good priest. Yet he never changed his conduct in the least, and Father Losa had recourse to the method of putting before him, from time to time, all such articles as he thought might be needful, and then left it to Gregory to choose whatever he pleased.

Father Losa was of opinion, that the peculiar feature of Gregory's poverty, was that God seemed to have willed that he should live only on the leavings of others. He was induced to draw this conclusion from frequently observing, that whatever was prepared purposely for him, either in the way of food or clothing, did him harm.

Long experience taught him that these illnesses could not be the result of chance, but arose out of a law made for him by God, the transgression of which, either by himself or by others, was followed by punishment, as regularly as an effect flows from its cause. At first he thought the food prepared for him might be too coarse, and had in consequence ordered more delicate meats to be given him. These also produced the same debility as the coarser fare to which he had been accustomed. Gregory himself then begged him not to allow anything to be made specially for him. But Father Losa, thinking that he made this request, in order not to be a burthen to anyone, caused some food of another kind, which he deemed more suitable to Gregory's health, to be dressed and served up, without letting him know that it had been prepared specially for his use. Gregory, however, discovered by the sickness which seized upon him after he had taken it, that it was designed for him, and then disclosed to his friend that it was God's Will that nothing should be made specially for him.

It was likewise remarked that any cloth or linen, or other material, bought for his use did him harm. This was at once apparent, although Gregory might, at the time these articles were given to him, be actually labouring under some grievous bodily ailment; for the sickness superadded by the articles designed for him, was evident to all eyes as something distinct and apart from the malady from which he was already suffering. So convinced was he himself upon this point, that in his last illness, when some particular things were requisite for his use, he begged of Father Losa not to procure them for him solely, but if anyone bestowed them as an alms to accept them.

It is not at all improbable that his death was hastened by certain remedies, prescribed and prepared specially for him by some devout and learned persons, who knew not of this peculiar cross which God had imposed upon him.

Thus we see that throughout the whole of life, God acted as his steward, portioning out for him everything he required, and so managing his affairs that He did not suffer him to waste any of his heavenly patrimony in the perishable goods of this world. Father Losa said to him one day: "God has treated you very rigorously in the midst of trials and difficulties. Hence it cannot be said of you: 'Thou hast eaten the good things of the earth.'" Gregory answered: "That is quite true, and as God doth, so do I desire." Truly it is on such occasions that man's spirit is tried and a proof given, whether it be of God, and filled with Divine sentiments, or simply of the world, and filled with worldly views and mercenary expectations, serving God like a hireling for the hire's sake, and deserting from His service when that pittance is seemingly withdrawn. But when, under the pressure of trials sent from above, a man courageously endures them, he shows that he is a worthy and faithful servant, deserving the commendation and love of his Lord and Master.

CHAPTER X.

MORTIFICATIONS AND SUFFERINGS.

THESE are two words, which affect various people in various ways. Some are frightened by them. Before others, they raise up visions of what they would call "dreamy mysticism," which ought, say they, to have no existence in this matter-of-fact world. In others they excite a certain amount of contemptuous pity for those who practise them, as deluded mortals, and "peculiar people," who are several centuries behind the age in which they live. These, for the most part, are men of the utilitarian school, who are credited, by those who know no better, with more common sense than nature ever bestowed upon them. Ignoring, or forgetting the fact, that we are living in a fallen world, and are members of a sinful race, condemned to a life of trial, they maintain that it is man's duty, they would almost say his sole aim, to obtain as much pleasure out of life and the things of this world as can possibly be extracted. But there was One Who said: "Deny yourselves, take up your cross, and follow Me." To pretend, therefore, to be followers of Christ without self-denial, or mortification, is to aim at sustaining a character, one of whose essential notes is left out. Hence all those who have tried to imitate Christ's example, and who, by the help of grace, have succeeded in so doing, as far as it was possible for human nature to succeed, have ever practised and held in the highest esteem, these two means of sanctification, which so terrify the effeminate world. They have always mortified their flesh, and patiently endured the pains and inconveniences to which that bitter ordeal subjected them. Gregory, therefore, was not behindhand in this respect; but, on the score of involuntary suffering, the infirmities sent him by God were almost continual. His first act after entering upon his life of solitude, was to kneel down upon the earth, and discipline himself with great severity. God, however, was not pleased to leave him, in this particular, entirely in his own hands, but seems to have told him, by a secret inspiration, that He Himself was to be his guide in mortification; for these words of Christ to St. Peter, were flashed suddenly and without any premeditation into his mind: "Another shall gird thee, and lead thee whither thou wilt not." To Gregory they were as the voice of God, saying to him: "It is for Me to draw the cords tightly round you; for you must walk according to My pleasure, not according to your own." A practical proof that such was henceforth to be his lot, was not long in presenting itself. For almost immediately, occasions of mortification and suffering began to pour in upon him, by reason of the many and painful ailments with which he began to be afflicted. Besides these, he was op--

pressed with the numerous labours which God moved him to undertake, and by the great inconveniences to which He willed him to subject himself. Added to these were those inward trials, which surpassed the others in their keenness and duration. Yet, he bore them all, with a courage and constancy more than human. These internal trials were of such a nature, that his endurance was put to its utmost tension, and "the burthen laid upon him seemed greater than he could bear." So deep an impression did the mental torture he endured at this period of his life, burn into his soul, that he could never afterwards recall it without a species of shuddering horror. What the nature of his trial was, no one ever knew, nor could he be induced to tell it; but, from the direction he gave to those who were suffering from spiritual desolation, it could easily be gathered, that he spoke with the precision and certainty of one who had had a long and practical experience in all such matters. Father Losa says, that while speaking with him on one occasion about the painful nature of these crosses, Gregory said to him, à propos of the matter they had been considering: "Father Losa, there are men who carry a load thirty times heavier than this." It is very easy to understand how such was the case with Gregory himself. For if we bear in mind his vehement desire to keep his soul free from all stain, and wholly occupied with chaste thoughts and fervent prayer, we may form some idea of the pain, which a whole troop of foul, polluting thoughts and filthy images would cause in one, before whose mind the devil could conjure up pictures of evil, more seducing even than the very reality itself. Although God gave him grace to trample under foot, the asp and the basilisk, yet it must have filled his soul with anguish unutterable, to feel by how slender a thread his will was held fast to God, especially since, on such occasions, the eyes of the spirit are opened, to see with greater clearness the dangers amid which the soul is walking, in order, no doubt, to make the highly spiritual man live with greater humility and circumspection. Another source of anguish in trials of this nature, is the reflection, that the enemies against whom we have to contend, are never wearied by the conflict, and rest not either day or night. Our stubborn resistance does not put them to flight; our virtue does not cover them with confusion. But this is not all. The war has not only to be waged with those who attack us from without, but there is need of still greater circumspection and dogged determination against those who assail us from within. Gregory stood proof against all this, and, though painfully tried, still contrived to find a source of joy in everything, because he knew that in proving his valour against God's enemies, he was contributing to the glory of his Lord and Master. Severe and terrible was the onslaught made by the devil against his faith, which, being the very foundation of the spiritual life, was specially attacked by the evil one, who sought to uproot and tear it from the centre of his soul. He tried to effect this by endeavouring to involve him in a maze of doubts, both by piling up all the improbabilities, which unaided human reason sees in the teaching of the Church, and by laying for him snares innumerable, and most cunningly contrived pitfalls, which would, without doubt, have entrapped any one, except a very wary and experienced soldier of Christ. Gregory, however, strong in faith and deeply founded in humility, would not enter the maze into which the devil desired to lead him, but walked securely in the light of Authority, which God's Church set before him, to shine like a pillar of fire, and to be a guide to his steps in the dark night of this life. But what will very likely seem strange, and even preposterous, in the eyes of some people, is the fact that holy men are not unfrequently molested in their retirement by temptations to horrible blasphemy. Such was the case with Gregory; but, knowing well how to meet the enemy, he always worsted him, and acquired great virtue from such encounters. A species of spiritual languor or faintness is another foe with which he had at times to contend. In this state, a feeling of weakness, and inability to advance one step forward, seizes upon the soul. There is apparently no nerve, no vigour in the man; but a limp, helpless, imbecile sort of sensation comes over, and seems to take possession of his whole being. To stand still, is to go backward in matters pertaining to the spiritual life, and this knowledge, coupled with the inability to push forward, was a source of great pain to one who, like Gregory, was so ardently desirous of carrying out God's Will with the utmost exactitude. He received, however, from his Divine Master the courage to bear this patiently, and not to faint under his tribulation, but, by perseverance and humility, to await the return of vigour from the same Divine Source, to which he thus learned to attribute, and instantly refer, all the graces and power which flowed thence into his soul.

The high degree of charity at which the perfect arrive, is another occasion of acute suffering to them; because, owing to the love they bear to God and to their neighbour, they are keenly alive and sensitive to whatever offends the Majesty of the One, or injures the spiritual or temporal welfare of the other. Words, therefore, can give no adequate idea of the grief which wrung Gregory's soul with anguish, when he contemplated the blindness of sinners, the obstinacy of conscious heretics, and the thousands of souls which are consequently lost every day. And though he deplored these spiritual evils, which make the world a place of the most intense suffering to holy men, he was by no means insensible to the temporal misfortunes, on account of which it justly bears the name of the " Valley of Tears."

When anyone was oppressed with sickness, or suffered an injury; when famine carried off the poor, or war brought grief and despair into homes, where women sat listening for footsteps which would never return, he was afflicted, not as if the calamity had befallen some one near and dear to him, but as if it had fallen upon himself. Like most men who are trying to be perfect, and carry out in their lives the suggestions of the Holy Spirit, he had to struggle against vain fear and forebodings of evil, with which such are molested, particularly in the beginning of their conversion. The dread of what the world will say or do, when they are seen aiming at something higher and nobler than the ordinary run of men, fills them with a vague apprehension. They are constantly troubled with the idea that persecution, resulting from the malicious and slanderous reports of the wicked, is impending over them, and that their conduct thus represented, will prove a stumbling-block to those whom they ought to edify. Though these fears may seem chimerical, and the result of an over-strained imagination, it is perfectly certain that they are oftentimes permitted by God, in order to try His servants; and, trivial as they may seem, what Father Losa says of them in his own quaint way, is quite true: "When the adversary tightens the cord in this way, he makes the servants of God to sweat for many hours together." Gregory, enlightened by God, and strengthened by His grace, met these attempts of the devil with that unconquerable patience and submission to God's Will, whereby he put to flight this malignant enemy, and learned in the midst of this trial, lessons of wisdom, or, we should rather say, strategy, by which he was able, in after years, to teach others how to outwit and defeat the cunning destroyer of souls.

In all these various phases of the spiritual life, it was observed by those who, like Father Losa, had opportunities for being certain of the fact, that Gregory never rested, or seemed to be contented in any one of the stages through which his soul passed. He was ever striving to push forward, to go higher and higher. This unshaken constancy can be attributed to no other cause, than to his continual acts of the love of God and of his neighbour. Father Losa, observing this, one day said to him: "Tell me, is it a fact that you neither rest, nor are able to rest, in the spiritual way?" Gregory answered: "It is quite true that I neither rest, nor can rest, while my brethren are in so many dangers and troubles. For it is not fitting that I should attend to my own safety, leaving them upon the bull's horns. I will not do so base a thing. If I know that but one of them is in danger, I will not rest my life long."

All this is very admirable, and shows how far Gregory had advanced in the way of perfection; but what strikes us as far more worthy of wonder, is the little account he made of those consolations granted by God to His faithful servants, by which, very often, they are enabled to mark their progress along the path to heaven. It must not, for a moment, be supposed that he made little of them or despised them, nor must we be considered as teaching anything else, than that they are to be highly esteemed. Far from it. They are God's gifts. They are means to attract and keep men in the way of virtue. But all that Gregory meant by not setting store upon them, was that he might serve God for His own sake with more purity of intention; and all that we would inculcate is, that they do not constitute the spiritual life, for, if so, how few of us could aspire to be spiritual!

Moreover, he never consoled himself with the remembrance of dangers past, nor with the thought of the virtues he had acquired. Like St. Paul, he looked not on what he had left behind him, but ever stretched forward to grasp what was to come; having an eye rather for what yet remained unaccomplished, than for that which he had, by his labour and industry, already built up. His watchword was, "Forward;" his aspirations ever, "Higher and higher." God satisfied his desire in both these respects, by leading him further and further along the road to perfection, and at the same time raising him higher and higher in the regions of spirituality. Hence the meaning of the few words he once said to Father Losa: "In the first years of my solitary life, God made me climb up some very craggy mountains." For, during his life, God made him pass through two purgatories of the spirit. The first came upon him when he was living at Guasteca. It was one of love. Those who have had even a slight experience of it will easily understand the grievous pain it causes; but such as know not even what it is to love God, will not be able to form any conception of the martyrdom through which it makes those pass, whose hearts are on fire and burn with its consuming heat. The light infused into the superior part of the soul by this love, wounds it so deeply, that no words can express, either the sweetness or the grief, which it causes to well up in the centre of the heart.

> "Nec lingua potest dicere
> Quid sit Jesum diligere."

A faintness comes over the soul, which makes it swoon away, because that is not granted which it loves so vehemently; and since this cannot be granted, at least perfectly, in the present life, an insatiable longing, a holy impatience, seizes upon all its powers, and while this lasts, there can be no ease or repose. It is while the soul is in this state, that God frequently inspires it with some of His own admirable wisdom, which finds expression in words conveying power and light to the souls of other men. Great is the pain endured by endeavouring to conceal the torments suffered, as well as the exceeding great joy wherewith the soul is flooded. Hence we may learn the extreme mortification which this holy man underwent, because throughout the whole time of his trial, he was as calm and silent as if he suffered not a spiritual martyrdom. The second purgatory was one of desire. His inability to attain to that Sovereign Good which he longed for so ardently, constituted this state of suffering. Figure to yourself a man, so enlightened by heavenly wisdom as Gregory undoubtedly was ; his understanding was expanded and quickened, to take in and grasp the great good proposed so clearly to him by a very lively faith ; his pure soul put no obstacles in the way of his will, which thus flew to plunge itself into the ocean of God's perfections, almost with the impetuosity of a disembodied spirit, that has looked for the first time upon the loveliness of the Divinity. Keep this before your mind, and you will have some idea of the intensity of his desire to possess the Supreme Good. The knowledge that he could not do this as long as he was in the body, inflicted upon his soul a mortal anguish, grievous beyond the power of words to express.

However, the greatest mortification of all, not so much by reason of its intensity as of its duration, was that which he imposed upon himself by his determination in everything to follow the lead of grace. Let us bear in mind, that this cannot be done without abandoning nearly everything that is pleasing to nature. Consequently, it will be easy to estimate the pain and inconvenience suffered by this servant of God, who had thus entered into an agreement with his soul, to check and deny himself in all things. For every-day life furnishes very many occasions, in which one who has resolved to follow such a course, will find opportunities in abundance to feel the weight of the Cross and the smart of the thorns. This would naturally enough be the result of such a determination; because grace very often requires of us what is contrary to the desire of nature. When these two are brought into conflict, one or the other must of necessity yield. Both cannot hold dominion in the same heart. Gregory, consequently, ever laboured to become as one who was dead to all creatures. Nature, on the contrary, would ever wish to be alive to them all. It seeks to be esteemed and honoured for whatever it does. There is nothing it dreads more than the disdain of men, and it counts no sacrifice too great to avoid it. Knowing well the enemy against whom he had to contend, this servant of God tried to hide his virtue and excellence, and shrank not from being despised by the world as Christ was. He divested himself of the cares inherent to temporal things, that he might be more free to seek and serve God. As nature is proud in the time of prosperity, and dejected in the time of adversity, it became one of Gregory's aims to receive with an evenness and constancy of mind, whatever it should please God to send him. Hence he did not seek for what might gratify himself, but simply and solely for what would redound to the honour and glory of his Lord and Master.

Nature is ever talking of self; that hateful word, "I," is always on its lips. When injured, it hates. When others are humbled, it rejoices. Gregory, on the contrary, always loved and wished well to those, who, either through malice or ignorance, opposed him. If they met with any adversity, he felt it keenly, and prayed to God for them, that He might pour down upon them His choicest blessings. By this means, he every day overcame himself more and more, and advanced in perfection, hungering and thirsting after God with so much ardour, that nothing else could satisfy his craving. Vigorously did the athlete of Christ breast, and toss aside the billows of this world's pleasures; never flagging, never drifting with the onward sweep of its mighty current, never sinking beneath its seething waters, but ever striving with all his might to reach God, Who stood waiting for him in the place of rest, to give him the crown prepared for the victors who strive manfully and lawfully to gain it.

It was while Gregory was living at Santa Fé that Father Losa discovered, or, rather, caught a glimpse of the manner of prayer whereby he continually entertained himself with God. The good Father had observed, that for many days his holy friend was looking very weak, and pale beyond the ordinary whiteness of his complexion. On this account he began to visit him oftener, and to stay longer in his company, trying by that means to discover whether he could afford him any relief. After asking for a long time, in vain, to know what it was that thus grievously afflicted him, he at length prevailed upon him to disclose the cause of his weakness and general debility. It appeared then, on Gregory's own testimony, that besides several very severe maladies which were, so to speak, domesticated with him, he had for a long time been tortured with very violent pains in his teeth. Father Losa was not satisfied with this explanation, but feeling convinced that these were but a tithe of his sufferings, importuned him still more, to tell what was the great cross that weighed him down. Then Gregory did what he had never done before :—he began to pray aloud to God, and thus manifested somewhat of that converse with which he was accustomed to entertain himself with his Maker: "Thou knowest well, O Lord," said he, "that for love of Thee, I neither have suffered, nor do suffer any creature to have a place in my heart! Why then, good Lord, dost Thou in this manner hide Thyself from me? How canst Thou endure to see me oppressed with so many maladies, and being able to cure me, dost not do so, but will have me seek the herbs that beasts do feed upon, and being able to heal me with a 'fiat,' wilt not do so?"

It is quite certain that Gregory spoke these words, not so much to ease his afflicted spirit, as to instruct his friend. Yet it was such an unusual thing for him to allow what passed inwardly between himself and his God to be seen by men, that Father Losa immediately wrote down the words he had uttered, that they might serve as an example of how we ought to represent our woes to our Heavenly Father, instead of bewailing them before our fellow-creatures, who, far from being able to lighten them for us, are very frequently disgusted by our selfishness in thus intruding our miseries upon the public notice of the world.

CHAPTER XI.

MORTIFICATION OF THE SENSES.

THE senses are the gates of the soul. Any one therefore, who wishes to preserve tranquillity within himself, must carefully watch them, and allow nothing to enter which might cause disturbance in that little kingdom, where man ought to reign supreme. There are, however, certain things in the visible, and there are certain beings of the invisible world, who are hostile to the soul of man: the former induce us to open the gates, the latter lie in wait for the moment when they are open, to rush in and lay waste the kingdom of the soul. Hence prudence requires, that they be carefully shut against these incursions.

This closing of the senses against alluring and dangerous objects is, therefore, the first and necessary step in the practice of mortification. The next is, to keep them closed against such objects even as are lawful, in order by this strict, and what may seem superfluous vigilance, the mere danger of ingress may be made very remote. A man so careful to mortify his interior as Gregory, failed not to be rigorous with himself in point of external mortification. Hence the general impression among those who knew him, was that he never took one step to delight his eyes with the sight of objects, which fill the senses of other men with pleasure. Thus, during the whole time he lived at Guasteca, where there are some beautiful springs of water, which are the chief attraction for the people of the whole surrounding country, he went out only once to look at them; and even on that solitary occasion he did it, not to derive any satisfaction from the sight, but simply to please Father Losa, who importuned him very much, and at length prevailed upon him to go. During a stay of several months in Mexico, he never left the house, except to go to the church which was but a few paces distant; and though almost entreated to visit a convent of holy Religious, he could not be persuaded to do so. When he had to go to Santa Fé, he left Mexico before day-break, that he might deprive himself of the gratification of seeing the streets and public buildings. In the little village of Santa Fé, there was attached to the very house in which he lived, an excellent garden which was quite a curiosity on account of its pleasant situation, the beautiful stream of water which ran through it, the taste displayed in the arrangement of its walks and flower beds, and the rarity and variety of the plants and fruits with which it was adorned. Yet for six whole years, he never once so much as cast his eyes upon it.

At length for the space of perhaps a year, he occasionally went out into it, to fetch a little water for his own use. Upon men, however, he was accustomed to look with a holy freedom as if they had been souls without bodies, or inanimate pieces of marble. He was naturally very fond of music, yet all the time that Father Losa knew him, he never went to hear any, though he had but to take a few steps from the spot where he lived, to have heard the most excellent that could be found. This no doubt led the good Father to question him, at times, upon this, as upon so many other points; for he tells us that Gregory, in answer to something he had been saying, declared that if the music of the Cathedral of Toledo, or even the choicest this world could boast, were but one step from his door, he would not go to hear it. This self-denial did not prevent him from appreciating any pieces, at the performance of which he chanced to be present. He listened to them quietly, and from them drew something which cherished the love of God in his heart.

The sense of smell, about which men in general are so fastidious, was also strictly guarded and mortified by this servant of God. He was a man, so constituted, that any bad smell caused him more than ordinary inconvenience; and yet he studiously avoided all odours that were sweet, and never made use of them. Hence though the most beautiful and sweet-smelling flowers were offered to him very frequently, his practice was gently to refuse them, except in cases where he saw that such refusal would pain those who made the offering.

In point of taste, one of his first resolutions on retiring into solitude, was never to eat for pleasure, but simply and solely to preserve life. This resolution he kept unbroken to the end of his days. His good friend and faithful companion once asked him to partake of a melon, some figs and a few grapes which he had procured for him. Gregory took a bit of the melon, and after smelling it, said: "It is enough for this year to have smelt this melon." When pressed to take some grapes, he tasted one, and said: "It is enough for this year," and after eating half a fig, he made the same remark. He was not led to do this because fruit disagreed with him; on the contrary, no food suited his constitution better, and it was an opinion of his, that fruit was the proper food for man, since he had been destined by God to eat of it in the earthly Paradise. "Never," said he one day, while speaking on this subject, "did fruit disagree with me." When Father Losa expressed some surprise at this, Gregory made what seems to us an answer containing a little quiet fun at Father Losa's expense: "The reason is," said he, "because *I* always eat moderately thereof." What formed his staple article of food was bread, the chief sustenance of the poor. But even in eating this, God suffered him to find great mortification. For years before his death he could not swallow a morsel, unless it were moistened by being dipped in soup, without salt or fat, or any condiment whatsoever. Oftentimes he would keep the bit he was eating in his mouth, and when told by Father Losa to swallow it, he answered: "I cannot find a passage for it." For him truly the greatest mortification was eating, as he frequently remarked, though none valued the unimpaired use of the senses more than he, because it afforded a most excellent means to a spiritual man for the exercise of christian mortification.

There was another method of mortification used by Gregory, which is probably neither well known nor much practised, from which he derived great profit. Everyone is well aware how the spirit is relieved by the sensible manifestation of its joys and its sorrows. Thus, it is a relief for anyone who has received a wound, to give vent to the anguish he suffers, by sighs and groans. So also is it in the case of great joy; the pleasure is enhanced by communicating it to others, or by expressing it with our bodily senses. In grief too nothing so relieves the overburthened heart as a copious flood of tears. Now in all the years during which Father Losa lived in the same house, and sat at the same table with him, he never saw him do anything, except on the occasion already mentioned, whereby he could discover his interior sentiments. He did not, in his intercourse with God, sigh or weep, or lift up his hands. All his exterior deportment was as calm as if he were occupied with nothing of any moment. Anyone who knows what prayer is, and how much the spirit moves the body to join in manifesting what it feels, while conversing with its God and Maker, will understand how great command over his whole being the continual practice of mortification had given to him. Father Losa, thinking this rather extraordinary, supposed the reason of it to be, that Gregory was so absorbed in the presence of God, that he could neither sigh, nor weep, nor speak. Having one day asked him if this were the case, he received the following answer: "No, Father Losa, that is not the reason, for I do groan and sigh thousands of times, and talk with God; but I do all this mentally. For thirty years I have acted thus, and my motive is, not to give nature any share in these feelings, since she is so false and treacherous. This is no small mortification to her."

Naturally enough, Father Losa tried to imitate his spiritual master in this particular, and so had some experience of its difficulty. For when he went, as he sometimes did, into the garden to pray, he could not prevent himself, in the fervour of his devotion, from sighing and lifting up his eyes and hands towards heaven. Then Gregory would say to him, gently and playfully: "Give nature a little refreshment, Father Losa, lest she die of hunger." Yet, much as he practised this species of mortification himself, he did not prescribe it to others, but allowed them to indulge in external manifestations of piety, knowing well that they are helps, and that most men cannot do without them. From what has been said on the score of mortification, one may see that Gregory did not go into solitude to lead an easy and indolent life. Such things as we have mentioned, require the continual coöperation of the spirit, and are as wearisome to the body as the severest manual labour.

The result of the rigorous treatment to which he subjected himself, was the acquisition of vast power over all his spiritual enemies. His courage in meeting them was so great, and his skill in putting them to flight so unfailing, that he scattered them as easily as the wind scatters the autumn leaves. He never lost an inch of ground in any contest. Confiding in God he was never dismayed, though assaulted by an entire host of temptations; and in the midst of their desperate assault he lost not a moment of time, but continued his exercise of the love of God and of his neighbour. His peace of soul was so profound, his self-mastery so complete, that no eye could detect whether he were in conflict, or in the enjoyment of peace. Being always the same, he verified that saying of Solomon, and frequently had it on his lips: "The wise man continueth like the sun." Lastly, God made him, so to speak, the defender of his brethren, the leader of their hosts against the devil, and, not unfrequently, received his struggles for them, as if they themselves had been personally engaged in the conflict. Gregory derived all this strength,—which enabled him so perseveringly to fight against the powers of evil,—from the lively faith and loving trust he had in God. He knew well and was feelingly convinced that our Heavenly Father will never allow us to be tried beyond our strength; and hence he fought against all the evil suggestions of the enemy, with the greatest rational pleasure. "When a man," said he, "begins thus to be a soldier of Christ, it is evident that he has ceased to be a child, and has cast aside the things that mark the period of childhood. He stands before his Maker no longer an infant, but in every sense of the word—a man."

CHAPTER XII.

HIS SPIRIT OF PRAYER.

FATHER LOSA was of opinion, from much that he had heard, as well as from personal observation, that this great servant of God had begun his life of prayer, almost as soon as he had attained the years of discretion. Gregory himself had given him cause to form such an opinion from having once said: "God called me very early to the use of prayer. In fact, I may say that in the ordinary acceptation of the term, I never was a child, and after having once begun this holy exercise, I never went one step backward in it." Now, if it be borne in mind that he never uttered an idle word or attempted to exaggerate the truth, we may safely conclude from his words, that from the very dawn of reason, he had begun to pray, and to give up his entire being to God. How perfect that prayer was, even in his childish days, may be learnt from what he told his biographer concerning that period. He said that when he was a page at Court, he used to be engaged almost continually in mental prayer. When sent from one part of the palace to another with a message, or with some little commission for the lords or ladies who happened to be staying there, he went about these matters with the same recollection and interior peace, as he did in the decline of his life, after having exercised himself in prayer for many years. In the midst of that gay and naturally distracting society, he never suffered any great dissipation to seize upon his spirit. Dukes and grandees came with their gorgeously attired retinues, and their motley group of followers, but they made no impression upon him. He was as quiet and collected, as if he were living in the solitude of a mountain, far removed from the noise and turmoil of the city. This great power, great even in those days, increased more and more as the years went on, till it became such as we have seen it towards the end of his life,—a species of almost uninterrupted contemplation. We may, therefore, argue that if at twelve years old, his prayer had attained such a degree of perfection, he must have begun to exercise himself in it at a very early age. We may also, with good reason, conclude that the time which elapsed between the age of twelve and that wherein he entered upon his solitary life, a period most probably of about eight years, was also spent in the exercise of prayer.

To his great perfection in this holy exercise must be attributed that constancy and courage, which he displayed during the two or three years he passed at Court, for the dangers he encountered during that short period, and the obstacles he overcame were such as could be fought against, and triumphantly overcome, only by more than human power, obtained from Almighty God, by more than ordinary excellence in prayer. An excellence of this nature is the result of a long practice in conversing with God. When we bear in mind that on Gregory's arrival in New-Spain, he could have been but little more than twenty years old, and was able even then to spend several hours a day in mental prayer, and to continue it while travelling, writing or conversing, our conclusion that he must have begun the practice of it at a very early age, is legitimate and well founded. The very means also which he employed when he arrived in Mexico for the acquisition of a more sublime degree of prayer, manifests a maturity and a solidity of virtue, which is the growth of many years. This was, to observe a most rigorous fast during an entire Lent, eating nothing the whole time but bread and water. In Gregory's case, it was not remorse of conscience for a disorderly and mis-spent life, which urged him to treat himself with so much severity. His entire youth was passed in the greatest purity and innocence. He had no fear of God, for being led by the way of love, all fear had been cast out of his heart. How powerful was the attraction of the love of God upon his soul, may be learnt from the fact that it drew him away from everything around which the affections of the heart entwine themselves. It loosed all those bonds which tie a man to his home and kindred. It drew him from his native land to a foreign shore. It made the splendour and riches of the new world lose all their brilliancy for him, and stripped them of all their power to charm and to attract. It drew him aside in the flower of his youth, into a desert place, that God might speak to his heart. During his life of solitude, this love of God perfected, and brought to their full maturity all the virtues of his soul. It taught him to bear with patience, and think nothing of the heavy burthens which God laid upon his shoulders for the trial of these virtues; and since God, in His loving kindness, always proportions to the strength of His children, the burthens wherewith He loads them, the greatness of those laid upon Gregory will give us a notion of his spiritual strength. They will show us that he spent the time which elapsed between the dawn of reason and his twentieth year, in bearing the yoke of the Lord manfully. Hence it fared well with him when God led him into His vineyard, and set him to do that work which He had marked out for him in this life. These words of the prophet Jeremias were, consequently, often upon his lips:—" It is good for a man to have borne the yoke from his youth."

What was the precise nature of that prayer in which Gregory exercised his soul during these first years of his spiritual life, could never with certainty be determined by Father Losa. We may take it for granted this was owing to no remissness on his part, in trying to discover it. But as Gregory was always very reserved about everything that concerned the workings of God within his heart, except when he saw that some positive good might be done to his neighbour by their revelation, we may be sure, he deemed it most expedient to say nothing on this subject. Father Losa, however, though not stating anything positively, ventures to suggest as most probable, that Christ our Lord was the theme of his prayer; because He is the foundation on which all spiritual life is built, as well as the gate through which every soul must enter into it. He was induced to put forward this opinion, from the fact that Gregory gave him frequent meditations upon the life of our Lord, and in particular on His Infancy and Childhood. These were so full of devotion, so methodical, so replete with the unction of the Holy Spirit, as to show they were the result of long and oft-repeated thought. He must also have occupied himself very often with considerations on the life and virtues of our Blessed Lady, for his words breathed a most tender and childlike devotion to her. He always strongly advised all who desired to make progress in the spiritual life, frequently to recite the Rosary, and to meditate upon the mysteries of which it is composed. Like all the great teachers of asceticism, he thought the existence of this devotion in any soul, a mark of aptitude for sanctity, and its absence an indication of a state, if not of actual spiritual death, at least of spiritual lethargy, which is the unmistakable forerunner of spiritual death.

CHAPTER XIII.

HIS PRAYER IN SOLITUDE.

AS far as we can discover, Gregory must have been close upon his twenty-first year, when he entered into solitude to lead the life of a hermit. With regard to the facts narrated in this portion of his life, we may be perfectly certain; because Father Losa in recording them, was not obliged, as in treating of his early years, to rely upon the reports and conjectures of others. Whatever he tells us about Gregory's solitary life, is the result of his own observation, and of conversations which he was in the habit of holding from time to time with his saintly friend. It is, therefore, less liable to errors and to exaggerations than the rest, for no man could live with another for upwards of eighteen years without knowing him thoroughly, and being able to correct any mistake into which he might have fallen by trusting to the narratives of others. It will be interesting, therefore, for us to learn from Father Losa, what was the prayer his friend made use of during this period of his life. The first in which he exercised himself in solitude, was expressed in these words: "Behold, O Lord, I enter upon solitude, only to serve Thee, without any regard to myself." By these words he offered himself to the Eternal Father, to be His slave, so that both his labours and whatsoever should result from them, might redound to His honour and glory. This is what he intended by the words, "without any regard to myself." Hence, his intention was to aim in all his works, solely at promoting the honour of God. An offering made with such goodwill was graciously accepted by our Heavenly Father, and as a kind of reward, the Divine Wisdom took upon Itself to be the holy man's guide and master in the difficult ways of the spiritual life.

The next stage of his prayer was one of resignation in all things to the holy Will of God. It consisted of these words: "Thy Will be done on earth as it is in heaven. Amen, Jesus." This indicates a very high degree of perfection; and perfection, moreover, which it is not easy to obtain. It imports that Gregory submitted his own will entirely to God in all things, desiring to do simply and solely what God should will to have done, and with as much completeness and readiness as it is fulfilled in heaven.

God permitted Gregory to continue in this exercise for three years. During that time, he repeated the words of this short prayer mentally, as long as he was awake, with almost every breath he drew. If we take into consideration how short his sleep usually was, and how extraordinary his watchfulness, we shall be able to make a calculation of the vast multitude of times this beautiful ejaculation rose from his heart to God. He told Father Losa, that after he had been employed in it for about a year, he did not observe his breathing, on account of his attention being given wholly up to excite his memory to the performance of this act, with all the fervour of his soul. If he ceased even for a moment, on the instant, a vast crowd of foul temptations rushed in upon him. The same thing happened if he took up a book to read; so that he was obliged in self-defence to adhere steadily, and without interruption, to this exercise appointed for him by God. It became for him an armour, which stood proof against all the fiery darts of the most wicked one.

Having had ample experience of its never failing efficacy, he cordially recommended it to others, as an impenetrable buckler of defence against the powers of hell. So completely did the energy with which he applied his soul to form these acts of resignation, occupy all his faculties, that he was elevated and carried out of himself beyond all the cares of this life. The proof of this lay in the fact, that though he was assailed by very violent temptations while engaged in this prayer, yet, when these had passed, he scarcely remembered them. Resignation to the Will of God was the very root of his spiritual existence. From it he drew all the vigour, the life, the power, and the energy of his soul.

When the three years, destined by God for his perfection in this act of resignation had elapsed, and his soul had come to be in most perfect conformity to the Divine Will, it pleased his Heavenly Master to advance him yet one step further in his onward course. He was now ready to enter upon that exercise, wherein perfection, such as it can be attained in this life, is found. This consists of the continual practice of that love, which is the comprehensive summary of the whole law given by our Lord: "Thou shalt love the Lord thy God with thy whole heart, and with thy whole soul, and with thy whole mind, and thy neighbour as thyself." In this he understood that he was now to employ his whole strength, and by one act,—in imitation of God,—to love both his neighbour and the great Creator of all things. He consequently, omitted the continual repetition of the act of resignation, which he had formerly used, and applied all his energy to elicit acts of love; understanding that a multiplicity of acts differing from each other, would serve only to distract and weaken him in the service of his greatest love. All the energy which he had formerly thrown into the acts of resignation, was now thrown into the act of love; or, rather, he felt his power increased by the love wherewith he was inspired; so that he could say with truth, that he found it a matter of great difficulty to forget, even for the shortest space of time, this act, upon which all the power of his being was concentrated. Hence he continued to elicit it, almost without effort, even while eating, or conversing, or performing any other action of mind or body.

It was in this stage of his spiritual life, that he began to read the Holy Bible with much greater assiduity, than he had been accustomed to do in the early days of his retirement. His studies in this Book of books, were now prolonged to as many as four hours every day. His love of God was the lamp which discovered to him the meaning of the sacred writings, and they reflected back again into his burning heart, the love, and mercy, and justice of which their every letter spoke. How advantageous to those who would lead a holy life, the frequent reading of this inspired Volume is, may be seen from the admirable effects it produced in Gregory. It gave to his words a weight which they did not possess of themselves. It clothed the answers he gave to various questions, with discretion, and made his counsels replete with a supernatural wisdom. It caused him to love his neighbour with the same measure of love with which he loved himself. It filled his heart with an extraordinary purity, gave to his prayer boundless liberty, and procured for him a dominion over his enemy, and a habit of mortification as great as that practised by the sublimest contemplatives.

His prayer also did not now need, so much labour as formerly, nor had he to use so great violence with himself in the performance of it, but the act whereby he made it, was more ethereal, more spiritual. It was also less sensible, that is, without so much aid from the sensitive powers as formerly, and was therefore far more perfect.

In this way, Gregory daily advanced higher and higher in perfection, proving in his person, that external occupations are by no means incompatible with the very sublimest spirituality. For even at the time when he had reached the perfection of his state, he used, as we have seen in his life, to attend somewhat to external occupations, to reading, to writing, and to a certain amount of scientific learning. Some very holy persons, on this account, were of opinion, that he was not as far advanced in spirituality as he actually was. Their preconceived notion, that such occupations are calculated, by their very nature to render a high degree of sanctity impossible, would easily lead them into this error. So far, however, were external occupations from being any hindrance to him, that in the last year of his life, he said to Father Losa: "My inner man doth work without imparting ought to the outer, and my conference with God is not now held in mental words, but in another language." Thus did he obtain that close union with God, and those heroic virtues, which made him an object of wonder and of reverence to all who either saw, or heard of his sanctity.

CHAPTER XIV.

ANSWERS GIVEN BY GREGORY, WHICH MANIFEST HIS SPIRIT.

WHEN a man, such as Gregory Lopez, can be induced to speak about himself, he will answer questions put to him with all the simplicity of a child. No false humility will lure him into excessive depreciation of his virtues, or concealment of his defects; but he will give utterance "to the thing which is;" that is to say, the truth. In him is verified, to the letter, that saying of the Great Master: "Out of the abundance of the heart the mouth speaketh." It is, therefore, in order to lay before the reader a clearer idea of Gregory's spirit, that we bring forward certain answers of his, made in reply to questions addressed to him on matters pertaining to his inner life. From these it will be easy to conceive unto what a height of perfection he must have attained.

Among the many admirers of his sanctity there was a certain Religious, who was remarkable, not only for his sanctity, but also for the wide range of his literary and scholastic attainments. He was a man whom Gregory highly esteemed, and to whom he opened out his heart more freely than to other men. In fact, he saw in him a spirit akin to his own, a man with aims and aspirations, such as filled his own heart, so that he could more easily disclose himself to him than to such as would not be able to appreciate what he said, or to enter into his views. This holy Religious, having heard, no doubt, of Gregory's unwearied application to prayer, and astonished perhaps at what may have seemed to him an impossibility, asked him if he had any fixed times, or particular hours during the day or night, in which he excited his flagging energies to greater exertions. He also desired to know, whether conversation, or offices of charity,—such as advising and comforting those who came to him for counsel in their difficulties and doubts,— had the effect of cooling the ardour of his love. Gregory's answers to these questions implied that he had no set time for renewing his flagging energies, and what is more, that he did not need any; because no created thing could disturb him, or take off his attention from that upon which his whole soul was engaged. His interior operations, he added, were always in perfection, since habit had made it quite natural for him to act as he did. Hence, he never went back from the perfection of that union, to which God had called him, but always continued to push forward. To it he attributed all that he knew; for books had not given it to him, but God. Yet it was a great consolation to him to find, that what he had learnt from God, was written in the works of Thaulerus and Rosbrochius,—and as for the holy Mother Theresa of Jesus, he was never tired of extolling her spirit.

This same Religious, thinking that Gregory's proceedings would have been different had he been in Holy Orders, said to him: " But if you were a Priest, what would you do?" "What I now do," answered Gregory. "How would you prepare yourself to celebrate Mass?" "Just as I now prepare myself to hear it," was the reply. "With regard to the *Mementos*, how would you make them?" "As I do always. And further: if I were to die within a few hours, I would do nothing more than I now do; for I am now actually giving to God all that I have; more I cannot give, unless He in His mercy bestow it upon me." This good Religious then said to him: "I have observed, that when the soul is loving God with all its strength, and is in the enjoyment of a delicious peace, the Divine Lover occasionally seems to draw aside the veil which hides Him from His child, and then the favoured soul, wonderfully dilated and quickened, is made capable of things which it can neither comprehend nor express. When, however, it would pause, and dwell upon the wonders God has wrought in it, these favours disappear, leaving only their sweetness behind. Now, tell me, my dear Gregory whether, after experiencing such goodness from the bounty of God, you retain a vivid recollection of it in your mind, or is your soul always at that height to which God only occasionally raises other men?" Gregory answered: "As it is not in man's power to procure such singular favours from God, so also it is not in his power to remember them, or to remain for any length of time in that state, wherein they are experienced. I doubt very much, whether any mere creature, with the exception of the Most Holy Virgin, remained always in so sublime a union. In the ordinary union, such as God has bestowed upon me, a man may both constantly persevere and even improve therein to an eminent degree." Continuing to speak on the same subject, he said: "Visions, revelations, ecstasies, raptures, and the like, are not the height of perfection, nor does perfection consist therein, though God, at times, grants them to such as are perfect. God works in every soul according to its capacity, necessity, and disposition; consequently, souls that are perfect and experienced in the act of a pure, simple, and perfect love, need not the suspension of their senses in order that God should communicate with them; for the senses neither hinder nor disturb the Divine communications. As for myself, I have never had any ecstasy, revelation, or rapture which deprived me of my senses, because these senses never cause me any distraction."

On another occasion, while discussing with Gregory, this Religious spoke of some holy men, who, being in a state of passive union with God, attained great peace and tranquillity. "Such as these," said Gregory, "are good souls, and in a good way; yet, perfection and merit, lie not in acts of enjoyment, but in the endeavour of the soul to employ all her forces in loving God in the most perfect manner, and with the most perfect act, of which it is capable. This, you see, is rather doing than enjoying, whereas the other is rather enjoyment than work. For the soul which loves God perfectly can give no more than she does; God requires nothing else from her, since in this consists the whole Law and the prophets."

Father Losa, in one of his numerous conversations with Gregory, was saying how acceptable to God, and in what high esteem with Him, those persons must be, who, with an ardent zeal, are continually praying for the Church, for the promotion of God's honour, and for the salvation of souls. In reply, Gregory remarked that it was a great perfection,—a perfection, moreover, which belongs to few. "I understand," he said, "that Mother Isabella of the Nativity, a nun of the Convent of the Conception at Mexico, but now dead, had attained to this perfection of which you speak." The Father says, that this holy woman learnt by revelation from God, that Gregory was continually occupied with the same exercise. For in one of her letters, wherein she speaks of Gregory, she wrote these words: "I am always engaged in that employment in which God hath put me, of praying for the whole Church, and thus also doth my Brother." Those who understand prayer, says Father Losa, maintain that these various kinds of prayer, wherein Gregory was so great a proficient, are more trustworthy proofs of sanctity than the gift of miracles; since they are a better indication of holiness than the power to do wonderful deeds, which has often been granted to very imperfect men.

CHAPTER XV.

OTHER KINDS OF PRAYER USED BY GREGORY LOPEZ.

NO matter how far advanced in sanctity any one may be, he is not, on that account, exempt from the assaults of his spiritual enemies. His life on earth is " a warfare," and though occasionally the battle rage not around him, it has not ceased altogether. Always, therefore, must he stand with his loins girt, and his weapons ready. When we are actually engaged in the contest, Gregory will teach us how to turn it into a prayer. Like us all, he had his combats to endure. But they never excited any fear in his heart. He faced his enemies like a valiant soldier, and took delight in fighting and routing them. When the victory was his, as it always was, he offered it up to God, together with the reward it had procured for him. He reserved nothing for himself. The power to fight, and the victory, came from God; to Him alone, therefore, be the honour and glory. His frequent victories raised in his heart a noble disdain for his foes. Whenever he saw them rising in vast hordes against him, he rejoiced, as huntsmen do when they see abundance of game, because an opportunity was thus afforded him of supplying his Master's table with great spoil. Nor was it simply the victory and its rewards which he offered up in sacrifice to his Lord. Profoundly convinced, and humbly acknowledging

Him as the foundation of all good, he also made an oblation of the strength whereby he had been enabled to bear off the palm of victory. Hence, also, whenever any favour was bestowed upon him by God, he instantly, without dwelling in the least upon the gift, carried it to the feet of his Master, and there sacrificed it, protesting in His presence, that of himself, he was nothing, and could do nothing, except indeed abuse the gift of liberty and fall into sin.

Another very excellent practice of his, was to offer up to God the passion and death of His Son, Jesus Christ. He used to do this sometimes for the whole world, and at others, for particular persons, or to obtain some special favour which he ardently desired, either for himself or for those who had recommended themselves and their necessities to his prayers. He attributed many of the favours granted him, to this most efficacious oblation, or spiritual Mass, as he called it. What countless blessings might we not obtain from our loving Father, if we had only a little care in His service! Here is a pious custom which might be practised, not simply when we assist at the Holy Sacrifice of the Mass, but at any moment of the day. We need only raise up our hearts to Him Whose ears are ever open to our aspirations, and by a few burning desires, tender to Him our most acceptable offering. Take up the holy practice, accustom yourself to it, and a speedy improvement in life and manners will be its immediate fruit in yourself, while, God alone knows, how many a poor sinner will owe his conversion to you, how many a struggling soul will gain the victory through your prayers, how many prisoners in Purgatory, sighing after the presence of God, will be loosed from their bonds by your work of love, and ushered into the glorious kingdom of heaven. Gregory said to Father Losa, when they were once speaking of this spiritual Sacrifice of the Mass: "God has thousands of priests in the world, who many times each day make this spiritual oblation. And as for myself, there are two kinds of spiritual communion I am in the habit of making,—one consisting of an ardent desire to receive Christ our Lord sacramentally,—the other to receive into myself the Father, the Son, and the Holy Ghost, that so I may become a living temple of the Most Holy Trinity, and give It an actual lodging in my heart, there to live and abide for ever."

When requested by Father Losa to tell the way in which he exercised the love of God and of his neighbour, he answered, that he did this by repeating a few verses of the Psalms, such as: "O all ye nations praise the Lord! Praise Him all ye people! O all ye works of the Lord! bless the Lord; praise Him and glorify Him for ever! Let all the earth adore and bless the Lord!" A prayer so full of fervour, so comprehensive, so brief, cannot fail to be acceptable to all loving hearts, and we trust that following the example thus given, many thousands of such acts will rise like incense before the throne of God, and become unto Him an acceptable sacrifice and an odour of sweetness.

The Holy Church was another object which excited all the love of his heart, and made him pour forth in her behalf many an efficacious petition to her Almighty Spouse. He longed that her sway might be extended over the whole earth, and that those who sat in the darkness of infidelity, as well as those who were infected with heresy, might be gathered into her bosom, protected there from the assaults of the devil, and finally presented to Jesus Christ as the children which He had given to her to bring up, till they attained the perfection of the manhood of Christ.

A practice of prayer which he recommended with much warmth, was that of praying for the conversion of great sinners. It is a charity which cannot fail to be very pleasing and dear to God, Who wills not the death of such, but that they should be converted from their evil ways and live. To incite others to a similar love for these lost sheep, he used to relate what had passed between St. Catharine of Siena and our Divine Lord. While engaged in earnest prayer for those who were living in the state of mortal sin, she heard from His sacred lips these consoling words: "My daughter, I entreat thee to pray to Me for these." This sentence of our Lord used to break from Gregory's lips with great fervour and sweetness, whenever the conversation happened to turn upon poor sinners.

In order to inspire others with the same sentiments of tenderness and compassion for them, he frequently narrated a passage, which occurs in the eighth Epistle of St. Denis the Areopagite to Demophilus, where he relates what he had heard from the mouth of the Bishop St. Carpus. It appears that an idolater had succeeded in perverting a newly-converted Christian, and caused him to apostatize from the faith which he had so recently embraced. The spirit of the holy Bishop was stirred within him, when the news of this defection was brought to him. Zeal for God's honour burnt in his breast, and, praying, he besought God to sweep them both away from the face of the earth. Looking up to heaven in the midst of his prayer, he suddenly beheld the form of the Man-God seated in glory, and surrounded by millions of bright angelic forms. Then, looking down upon the earth, he was filled with horror to behold, as far as his eye could reach, a seething, boiling ocean of liquid fire, bounded by dismal caves and rifted cliffs of red-hot adamant, against which the flaming ocean thundered its fiery billows, laden with the shrieking souls of men. On the brink of this ocean tottered the two poor wretches, against whom the Bishop had just uttered his prayer. They were pale with horror; pale, though the red glare of the fire beneath shone upon their blanched cheeks. Their eyes were starting from their sockets, and they clutched convulsively at the rocks, lest they should be snatched from their uncertain footing by the infernal serpents, which hissed at them, and opened wide their jaws to devour them. Carpus heard a voice telling him it would be well to pray for them, lest they should become a prey to the devils who already exulted over them, as if they were their own. But Carpus would not; on the contrary, he prayed that God would allow them to fall among their enemies, and be eternally destroyed. Lifting up his eyes, he then beheld what filled him with astonishment. He saw Jesus, with a mild and compassionate countenance, rise from His throne, and stretch forth His hands to help them. He heard Him commanding His Angels to rescue them; and then, turning towards Carpus, he uttered these words: "O Carpus! I am ready to suffer again for the sake of these! See whether you would wish to be eternally in this same hell, amid its lost ones, its serpents, and its fire, deprived eternally of the joys of God."

From examples such as these, he sought to fill all who came within the reach of his influence, with the mildness and sweetness of Jesus Christ.

In the prayer which he poured forth for others, his chief, his only aim was to obtain of God, that the Divine Will might be accomplished in them with as much perfection as it is in heaven; and from everything he heard he took occasion to make this petition to God. If, for instance, any one said: "The King of Spain is feared and respected for his power, and consequently holds his dominions in peace," he turned it into a prayer, and said: "Thou, O Lord, art all powerful, all just: may all men fear and reverence Thee, and mayest Thou possess this Thy kingdom in peace." When a father was praised in his presence for being good, and on that account, was said to be much beloved by his sons; he spoke thus to God: "Father and Fountain of all good things, may all Thy sons love Thee." Reflecting how the gardener labours to the utmost of his power, in order to make all his trees bear fruit, he would turn to God, and say,

"Creator of all things, let none of Thy creatures perish, but may they all yield Thee fruit in its proper season."

If accounts of wars reached him, in which there was great carnage, he would lift up his heart to God, and say: "Behold, Father, how Thy sons, and my brethren, whom Thou commandest me to love,—behold how they conduct themselves." In one word, everything, whether it was good or evil, became to him a motive of prayer.

He several times told Father Losa, that he saw all that was in the world, concentrated in one point in God; and this, too, without any process of reasoning. This, of course, was effected only occasionally, by some great light of contemplation, vouchsafed him by God. St. Gregory the Great explains how this may be brought about. "To the creature," he says, "who contemplates God, all creation seems small. And no wonder; for in that light the vast capacities of the mind are opened out, and acquire such expansion in God, as to be capable of grasping the whole world. The soul of him that is so enlightened is lifted above itself, and all its powers are enlarged, so that it easily grasps, what in its normal state, would be beyond its comprehension." It is no wonder, then, that Gregory, when raised by contemplation above sensible things, should have seen them all as one point in God. From this we must not imagine, as the great Pontiff observes, that heaven and earth were narrowed; but the mind of him that saw, being expanded by the contemplation of God, was enabled without difficulty to see all that was below him.

One of Gregory's most ardent desires was that others

might be brought to praise and offer up prayer to God in the midst of their external occupations; for, knowing the great advantages to be reaped from such a holy and commendable practice, he was eager that as many as possible might adopt it. Multiplicity of worldly cares and great stress of business, is no excuse to set aside this species of prayer; for the Machabees, in the midst of the anxieties of their numerous and difficult campaigns, and even amid the din of their bloody conflicts, while smiting the enemies of the Lord with their swords, had their hearts raised up in prayer to God.

Another practice of prayer, upon which he set great value, is worth mentioning here. Let us hope that many will take it up and reap from it all the fruit it is calculated to produce in them. This was to raise up his heart to God in mental prayer before he gave an opinion, or inculcated anything as worthy of being done by devout men; also when any one asked him a question, or again when he himself desired anything. By this he implored the aid of Divine grace, that his opinions might be sound, his counsel prudent, his answers full of wisdom, and his desires in conformity with the holy Will of God. In order to encourage others to do the same, he used to relate what the Holy Scriptures say of Nehemias, in the Second Book of Esdras: For when King Artaxerxes asked him what was the petition he wished to make to him, Nehemias first prayed mentally to God before he proffered his request; and God turned the heart of the Monarch graciously to listen to and grant all that he desired.

The prayer which above all others was honey to his lips, was the Our Father. He loved it greatly, because it was made by Jesus Himself, and had procured for him countless favours and graces. To each of its petitions he was in the habit of adding the words: "On earth, as it is in heaven." Thus, when he said, "Hallowed be Thy Name," he added: "On earth, as it is in heaven." It was in this way that he showed his zeal for God. Others manifest this by their writings, by undertaking labours and journeys, by exhorting others to virtue. But God does not lead all men alike, and hence Gregory was inspired by Him to show his zeal in a different way. Whenever, therefore, he wished to help his neighbour, he straightway betook himself to prayer, and laid all his wishes and views before God, knowing that all good comes from Him. Wonderful was the amount of good he effected in this way. He himself used frequently to say to Father Losa: "It is much better to treat with God than with men." This practice, however, did not prevent him from answering, by word of mouth or by letter, those who applied to him for advice in any matters of importance. There was nothing narrow in him; for while acting as he did, he never blamed the conduct of others, but frequently gave thanks to God, that there was no lack of good men in the Church, who assisted the great family of Christ in a totally different way from that in which he tried to do it.

CHAPTER XVI.

HIS ABIDING UNION WITH GOD.

GREGORY directed his will towards God, the Supreme Good, with so great an intensity, with so much singleness of purpose, and with such a persevering constancy, that his union with Him might almost be termed immediate. As we have said before, this was not effected, as in the case of many Saints, by raptures and ecstasies, but by his own intensity of purpose aided by Divine grace.

Father Losa goes so far as to term this union with God, a transformation into God. By this he means to say that his will, and his whole soul, was so united to the Divine Will that he could say with the Apostle: "I live, now not I, but Christ liveth in me." Those who knew him, and had the privilege of seeing his daily life, declared that he was a most Christ-like man. He esteemed nothing of any value, except what was spiritual; and when those who, like himself, ardently aspired after perfection were conversing with him, he eagerly and zealously urged them to aim at this spiritual transformation, using these words of St. John: "He gave them power to be made the sons of God; to those that believe in His Name; who are not born of flesh and blood, nor of the will of man, but of God." That this doctrine was never reprobated by any of the numerous spiritual persons who conversed with him, is a strong argument that there was nothing reprehensible in it. One of the effects of this immediate union with God, if we may venture to give it that name, is a great spiritual joy, which ascetical writers call *"fruition,"* because such as are raised up by God to so high a state of spirituality, do not so much seek God, as actually enjoy Him; they are with Him without any effort of their own, and are in that state called "PASSIVE UNION." For though, in such cases, the soul does in reality act, yet that action is not so much the seeking after, as the possession of, its Beloved. It exercises the act of enjoying more than that of desiring.

It cannot be stated with certainty that Gregory ever had any such union with God as this; for the Divine Lover never bestowed Himself so abundantly upon him as fully to satiate the desire of his heart. He always longed and aspired after more and more love. Hence his exercise consisted, not in enjoying what God had given him, but in eliciting burning desires that God would give him still more, and unite him still more closely to Himself. St. Denis the Areopagite says that his master Hierotheus had this state of spiritual rest, or fruition. He considers it the highest perfection attainable in this life. Most contemplatives are of the same opinion. Doubtless, it was on this account that Hierotheus had the name of divine given to him; for by this species of union, the soul is rendered most like to the Divinity, Which performs all Its operations without labour, in the fruition of Its own unspeakable perfections. Gregory was often told of this by Father Losa, and though he seemed from his thorough acquaintance with all its details, to have had experience of it, he yet deemed the state of action better for himself, and gladly chose it in preference to the more easy and sweet state of fruition. "God," he said, "had given him this exercise as the most suitable for him, and there seemed to be an injunction upon him to use all his power, and never to abandon it for any delight which might have resulted from the state of passive union."

Besides, he could not conceive how that state could be more perfect, which was less meritorious. For the active state, entailing more labour and difficulty, must consequently, be deserving of greater reward and glory, than that which is one of simple rest and enjoyment.

The transformation into Christ with which Gregory was favoured, consisted of an ardent love, in consequence of which he desired to follow Him in His life, and imitate Him in His Cross and labours. Christ's life, as we all know, was given to us by God, as a model after which we were to fashion our own, and so carry out the Will of God. For as He came, not to do His own Will, but the Will of Him that sent Him, so man's destiny and his perfection, consists also in doing this to the utmost of his power. He has, like Christ, to work the works of Him that sent him while it is day, that the night of death may not overtake him with that task unfinished. As, therefore, the life of Christ, from His birth to His death, was one continual bearing of the Cross, a life of bitter suffering and labour, it was Gregory's desire to imitate Him; and hence he wished rather for labour than for enjoyment. We may consequently look upon the fact of his being without sensible sweetness, as a particular privilege, whereby his desire was granted, thoroughly to resemble his Divine Master and Model. That such was the real reason of this privation appears from this,—that, though God did not bestow upon him those caresses which other holy persons have received, He yet gave him all the other striking favours, granted to such as are cherished by Him in that particular manner. He was endued with wondrous courage and constancy of purpose, evidently showing that God led him onward towards heaven like a man, and did not treat him as a child in spiritual matters. For, like a loving, gentle Master, He makes the entrance to the religious life easy and sweet to such as follow His invitation, and take His yoke upon them. As it is written in the Canticles: "He taketh them into His cellar, and giveth them to drink of His wine." He pours into their hearts light and joy, as a foretaste of what they shall have in heaven. And He does this, in order to give them courage to walk onward, boldly and perseveringly, to the very end. But when they have advanced some little distance, and are firm in their purpose to go on still further, He raises them to a higher degree of love, a love which is generous enough to suffer something for His sake. Of this treatment Gregory is himself a great example. At first "he tasted how sweet the Lord is;" presently, however, his love grew into a love desirous of suffering for his Beloved. So intense did it become, that its fervid heat almost wore away "the frail tenement of clay," and tortured him so keenly, that he sometimes said: "The martyrdom of whips, iron hooks fire, and sword, though full of suffering, nevertheless quickly passes away. But, besides such as testify unto God in the midst of material torments, there are thousands of spiritual Martyrs of great eminence." The lives of Saints and holy men will corroborate this statement, and convince any one, that to lead a holy life is a slow martyrdom, compared with which the short, sharp pang of a violent death, is very little. Paphnucius, the Hermit, seemed to think so; for, when taken and threatened with grievous torments unless he abandoned the faith, he smiled and said: "We hermits are accustomed to suffer such torments in the desert." Gregory was one of these spiritual martyrs; and so little did he fear death, and whatever torments there might be in the dread transit from this world of sense to the world of spirit, that he looked upon it rather as a release than a punishment, and met it, when his time came, with as much alacrity and pleasure, as men exhibit when they go forth to the amusements and the delights of life. "To me," he said, with the Apostle, "to live is Christ, and to die is gain." From this we may gather what was his spirit. It was a spirit of joy in suffering for Christ, and of delight and glory in the Cross. Like St. Paul, he could say: "Far be it from me to glory in anything, save in the Cross of my Lord Jesus Christ;" and with David also he could cry out, and say: "What shall I return to the Lord for all that He hath given to me?

I will take the chalice of salvation;" that is to say, I will drink of the chalice of His Passion. His pleasure was to suffer for Christ; and so far was he from looking for spiritual sweetness to compensate him in some degree for what he underwent, that this was a common saying of his: "Perfect souls are rather displeased, than otherwise, at having such consolations. For a man is offended if a bunch of grapes or an apple be offered to him, whereas a child is pleased with the same." "The present life," he used to add, "is not a life of joy and rest, but of sorrow and of labour."

From this rejection of all delight, even though of a spiritual nature, we may learn what Gregory's poverty of spirit was, the characteristic mark of which is, not to desire anything but God, and Him for His own sake. Perfection, therefore, is measured by this standard, and not by those gifts, such as sweetness, ecstasies, and the like. Gregory's whole aim in life was, consequently, to be always in possession of this intense charity or love of God, that he might thus be a perfect imitator of Christ, on Whom he fixed his eyes, as on some magnificent masterpiece, from which he was to copy, and to try to express in his own person the beauty he saw in the original. "Mine eyes," he used to say, "are ever on the Lord. And this with regard to Christ is the duty of every one who aspires to the title of wise." "The eyes of a wise man are in his head," which is Christ. The soul which has been touched with the love of God is like the needle of a compass,—ever true to the pole. Christ is its point of attraction, and towards Him it turns in every place and on every occasion. Those who were thus intent upon the great Model of men, were very dear, and their company very acceptable to him. Four such were specially dear to him; and one day, as they sat bareheaded at table with him, Gregory, looking at them, said: "Blessed be God, because all we, who sit at this table, have our heads uncovered." What he meant by these words was, that they were all spiritually looking on Christ our Head, Who was at that time manifest to them all. It is not at all improbable, that he saw into their souls, and was able, by the light God gave him, to read the secrets of their hearts. Many instances are recorded, and many more were known to Father Losa, in which Gregory showed by his words and actions, that this power was at times given to him. From these, and many other proofs, we may safely say that he never lost sight of God, and that God consequently ever kept the fatherly gaze of His providential care fixed upon him; for, as Job says: "He will not take His eye away from the just." This loving watchfulness of God over His servant, preserved him from being entrapped by the snares, or tripped up by the obstacles, the devil put in his path. "He gave His Angels charge over him, to guide him in all his ways. And in their hands they bore him up, that he might not dash his foot against a stone."

CHAPTER XVII.

THE EFFECTS OF HIS PRAYER.

IT was well known by all who were acquainted with Gregory, that God deigned to work by the prayers of His servant, many wonders which he, out of deep humility, studiously concealed. In this respect his secrecy was most profound. Those who shared his confidence on most other points, found him inexorably reserved upon this. His lips were sealed, and nought was ever gathered from word of his, that "He that is mighty had wrought great things by him." He could not have been personally ignorant of what God was effecting by his means, and hence his silence cannot be accounted for in this way. But with the instinct of sanctity, he knew so thoroughly that God is the Author of all good, and man simply an instrument, and an instrument, moreover, which greedily seeks to arrogate all the glory to itself, that he deemed it safer to hide what was being effected through him, than to expose himself to the peril of the insidious demon of pride.

Though Gregory was thus rigidly silent on what might add to his praise and redound to his honour, there is every reason for us to make known what fell under the observation of others. We shall, therefore, relate a few instances, where the effects resulting from his prayer, seemed marvellous to all.

While living at the Hospital of our Lady of Remedies, in the year 1579, there came to visit him a priest who was in great trouble. He had found out that the sacerdotal character is no absolute safeguard against the Devil and the heat of passion. He found the service of God a grievous burthen to him, and through the frailty of poor human nature, priest though he was, had stumbled and fallen. In him, the spirit indeed was willing, but the flesh was weak. He grieved over and blushed for his sins, and tried again and again to live a life conformable to the sacred character he bore. But occasions presented themselves, and he fell into the mire. Hearing of Gregory's great sanctity, he came and threw himself at his feet, and begged of him to point out some means to him whereby he might keep himself upon the narrow, rugged path which leads to heaven. He declared that he would do anything he told him, even though it were to retire to the mountain solitudes, and there lead the life of a hermit. Gregory's advice was given in a few pithy words: "Be for one year," said he, "a hermit in Mexico." Keenly appreciating all the meaning contained in these simple words, the priest returned to the city, and acting upon the advice he had received, succeeded in leading a very holy life. Going one day through the streets on an errand of charity, he suddenly felt an interior call to practice great recollection of soul. At the same moment he received so much strength and courage, that as he journeyed through the public streets and squares, though in the midst of the crowd, and deafened almost by its turmoil, he prayed and offered up the incense of his devotion to God with as much ease as if he had been engaged in such exercises for fifty years. He felt as though a new nature had been infused into him,—as if he had dropped all his old pursuits and thoughts of evil, and had been filled with those which lead to heaven. A marked change now occurred in his conduct. Before this, he had been a man fond of society, loving to mix with men, and taken up with the frivolous converse of worldly people. This, no doubt, had been the cause of many of his falls. But now he sought retirement, and found greater pleasure in treating with God and raising up his soul to Him, than he had ever before experienced in the fascinating society of highly bred and highly cultivated worldlings. Except when offices of charity called him forth, he was ever in solitude. Here he began to chastise his flesh by rigorous fasts, severe disciplines, and the use of the galling hair-shirt. God also permitted him to be tempted with great and terrible trials, some of which came from within, and others from without. But in the midst of them all, he had strength given him from on high, to bear himself manfully like a hardy veteran. He now began to lead a life of strict poverty, and, owing to the prayers of Gregory, there was formed within him, by the power of God, as perfect an eremitical spirit, as if he had been living for years in the desert. Molestations from the evil one,—and those too in visible forms,—were not wanting to render his life an exact counterpart of that led by some of the fathers of the Thebaid. At the end of the year he presented himself before Gregory, who was then at Guasteca, to give him an account of what had befallen him during that interval. He spent eight days in conference with him, and finally asked him what he was to do, now that the time appointed by him for this trial, had expired. The answer of his friend was brief, but pregnant: "Love God," he said, "and your neighbour." With that they parted. The priest, while journeying back to Mexico, began to ponder upon the words addressed to him. The precept of charity, he considered, he had already studied and practised sufficiently, and consequently he took himself to it again with rather a bad grace. But remembering what benefits obedience to Gregory's past counsel had brought him, he humbled himself, and began to see there was something more in the words than appeared at first sight. He resolved on the spot to make them the subject of his prayer, and began at once to ask God to reveal to him what lay hidden under the simple phrase. Soon a clear light shone upon his intellect, and an internal voice spoke within him and said: "To attain the love of God, you must divest yourself of all you are and have, and die to all things of the world." Immediately he made the oblation of himself to God, and felt that it was accepted, and that he now stood before Him, stripped of affection to all that might retard his approach. There was poured into his heart such an unction of divine love, that his understanding was neither able to comprehend, nor his heart large enough to receive it. He fairly languished away, and the wonder is that he did not fall from the horse on which he was riding. This incident served to show him the depth and perfection of

Gregory's counsel, and the mighty power of his prayer. He forthwith set about cleansing and enlarging his heart to receive and retain such a favour, and made a most steadfast resolution, thenceforth in everything to follow the Will and guidance of God. In this rapture of love he remained for seven hours, during which God revealed to him the beauty of the virtues, and caused him as it were experimentally to feel and to possess some of them. So profound was the impression made upon him by it, that for six years after he persevered, continually exercising the same act of love, and practising the virtues God had shown him. Even thirty years after this occurrence, the very recollection of it was sufficient to sustain, and give him courage to go on in the way of God, though beset on all sides with tribulations and afflictions of a very grievous nature.*

A man, evidently very desirous of advancing in spirituality, came to Gregory and besought him to become his guide, and to tell him what he had to do, in order to gain the height at which he aimed. "Go, Brother," said Gregory, "for Jesus Christ is your Master." The words poured a flood of light upon his soul. They struck him in a way he hardly deemed possible, and he began to advance with a spirit and a will which soon put him far on his onward way. He himself declared, that as great a change was wrought in his soul by those few simple words, as if he had been blind, and

* Father Losa wrote Gregory's life in the year 1598. This fact and several others were added to it about the year 1612, when it was first published.

had suddenly been restored to his perfect sight. He began to feel that man is nothingness, and Christ, the Truth, in very deed. He attributed the change wrought in him to the prayers which Gregory offered for his intention, and so powerful and efficacious were they, that they raised him to that state, wherein ecstasies and spiritual raptures are vouchsafed to the soul by God.

There was a religious woman of great piety, who felt an inward conviction, a sort of message from God, that a calamity of some kind or other was impending over, and would shortly fall upon her. Her heart was filled with anxiety, and a gnawing care, preyed upon it unceasingly, for the space of eight months. What she feared, was that this calamity might be a fall into some grievous sin. At last, after Communion on the feast of our Lady's Nativity, she felt a very strong impulse to recommend herself to the prayers of Gregory, who at the time, lived near Santa Fé. She availed herself of an opportunity afforded by a visit from a very holy man, who occasionally came to see her, to request him to carry her wishes to Gregory, and prevail upon him to pray for her. Her friend assented, and going to Gregory laid her case and her request before him. "I will do as she desires," said Gregory; "let her be faithful to God and fear nothing, for she shall not fall into any offence against Him." On hearing this answer, she was as much reassured, as if an Angel from heaven had come and spoken to her. What gave additional weight to the words of the holy man, was an incident which befell a pious Dominican in the city of Mexico. In the course of his journey to Santa Fé, the lady's messenger called at the Dominican Convent in Mexico, and there recommended the lady, for whose sake he was then journeying, to the prayers of the holy Friar. While praying for her intention, this Religious was rapt in spirit, and beheld Gregory kneeling in the presence of God and praying for her also, and the Divine Majesty graciously accepting his petition. It was in this vision that he first came to know Gregory Lopez, for he had never seen him before. The lady ever after entertained the greatest sentiment of veneration for Gregory, and did him many services. These he amply requited at the day of his death, for he procured for her just at that time, a very profound sentiment of God's immense goodness, and a clear perception of the world's hollowness, which set her heart on fire with Divine love for several days. When this happened she did not know that Gregory was dead, but in consequence of its coming upon her so suddenly and without effort, she concluded that he was gone to enjoy the presence of God, and was then pouring out prayer for her before the Throne of Mercy.

A priest who had a warm affection for Gregory, and followed his counsel in the way of prayer, received in consequence from God certain favours with which he was so pleased as to rest in them, without taking any pains to advance further in the way of the spirit. His friend Gregory quickly perceived this, and one day when they were together, quoted this verse from the prophet Isaias: "Thou hast found the life of thy hands, and therefore thou hast not asked." On hearing these words, his eyes were opened. He at once began to disengage his heart from sensible things and ways, and from that sweetness by which God had hitherto conducted him. He tried to the best of his power to divest himself of all affection to created objects, in order to be able with greater ease to obey the Divine Will, and carry out God's designs without hindrance. The result was a marked improvement, and a life of holiness spent with great profit to himself and to others.

A young man of very virtuous life and full of holy desires, was, for the space of some four or five months, greatly disquieted and disturbed in mind. His trouble arose from an uncertainty as to what state of life it were best for him to choose, in order to secure his salvation. In his distress he tried various means to put an end to the disquiet that reigned in his soul. He prayed earnestly, and asked others to pray for and with him. But all to no purpose. At length he thought of Gregory, whose fame had reached him, and at once determined to go to Santa Fé and see him. The mere sight of the holy man produced a wonderful impression upon him. It filled him with great reverence and peace. To look upon him had a soothing effect, and seemed to pour oil upon the troubled waters of his soul. In his interview with Gregory, he prayed him to ask God to enlighten him in his choice of a state of life; to point out to him one in which he might do Him most service, and then to give him the grace, cheerfully to enter upon and courageously to walk in it. When Gregory said to him: "Be at peace —I will recommend you to God," tranquillity entered

15

into his soul, and he was never again disturbed by a similar trial. Shortly afterwards, choosing the ecclesiastical state, he became a priest, and died with a great reputation for sanctity. He also deposed upon oath that when in later years, in the midst of his apostolic labours, he was afflicted with grievous and troublesome temptations, he used to go and expose them to Gregory, and always returned comforted and perfectly satisfied.

Another person went to visit Gregory for the purpose of obtaining his advice upon certain matters, and experienced during the fortnight he remained under his roof, some very fierce assaults of the devil. In the morning he told Gregory all that had happened, and was answered in the following words: "I forgot myself last night; you shall not suffer this henceforward." The next, and the following night, he found himself greatly relieved, and attributed his release from the attacks of the devil, to the prayers which Gregory offered up to God for him.

CHAPTER XVIII.

REVERENCE EXCITED BY HIS APPEARANCE.

THERE is a certain dignity, a certain nobility and refinement of look and manner, communicated by sanctity to those who are very holy, which attracts more attention, and inspires greater respect and reverence, than any merely human distinction either of birth or fortune. And this impression is produced in the minds not only of those who know that this is the result of God's grace, which shines even through the tabernacle of the body; but also in such as do not believe in any influence of that nature, and are consequently puzzled to what cause they ought to assign an effect which is before their very eyes. In a man like Gregory they saw a poor, solitary, unknown stranger, clothed in gray sackcloth, always bareheaded, lowly and humble in look; yet when they came before him, they felt that they were in the presence of no ordinary man. An involuntary feeling of awe crept over them, and those who could converse at their ease with princes and ambassadors, found themselves abashed before him, and felt as though they belonged to an inferior order of being. There was that in Gregory which filled all beholders with feelings such as these. It was not the virtuous only who experienced them, but those also who were worldly-minded and sceptical, and ordinarily little impressed by anything savouring of holiness or piety.

A man of high rank and at the same time of irreproachable character, was greatly disturbed by a matter of importance, upon the issue of which much depended. The suspense caused by awaiting the result deprived him of peace, and filled his soul with gloom. In his trouble he betook himself to Gregory to ask his advice and prayers. On presenting himself before him, he was so unmanned as to be unable to utter a word. Gregory waited some time to hear what he had to say; but no word passed his lips. At length he raised his eyes and looked at him, and probably recommended him to God. At that moment all trouble passed away from the gentleman's mind. Then Gregory began to speak of the matter about which the gentleman had come to treat with him, solved all his doubts and cleared up all his difficulties, though he had not heard one syllable about them from his visitor's lips. On going forth, he rejoined a cavalier who had accompanied him, and expressed to him his amazement that Gregory had understood his mind, and seen his very thoughts, before he had uttered a word; and then asked him if he could assign a reason why he had felt such perturbation and inability to speak, on presenting himself before Gregory. The other replied, that in his opinion, it was the sight of a man so venerable, so mortified, so holy, and so recollected, belonging rather to the court of heaven than to this world.

A student once paid him a visit, but without revealing the state of his soul to him, or even speaking a word about himself. Yet so great was the reverence and fear which took possession of him when looking on Gregory's face, that he determined to change his life, and altogether to reform his manners. This he did almost immediately, and eventually became a good and zealous priest.

A gentleman's servant was once sent with a message from his master to Gregory. On entering into the presence of the servant of God, he was seized with a species of terror and astonishment. So great was this that he could not utter a syllable. On leaving the house he said: "It is one thing to speak with men of the world, but it is quite another affair altogether to speak with this man of God. I never thought any man's face could cause me such trouble." Shortly afterwards he was sent to Gregory with another message, and when asked by Father Losa if he would like to deliver it himself, he excused himself, and said to the Father, who very probably enjoyed his discomfiture: "I had rather not! Pray, sir, do you do this for me!"

Very different were the sentiments which his appearance excited in the soul of another young man, who came from a great distance to visit him at Santa Fé. Hearing of his extraordinary sanctity, a great fear at first came over him, because he would have to present himself before one so illuminated by the wisdom of God, and so high in His favour. When, however, he actually came before him, all this trouble vanished, and so great a joy filled his heart, that he could not conceal it, but told Gregory what was passing within him: "Give God thanks for it," was all that Gregory said. Nor was this a mere passing emotion; it lasted for two days, during which his soul made great progress in spiritual things. He looked upon the fact of having been permitted to see Gregory, as an extraordinary favour; for it procured for him graces so wonderful, that he could hardly express in words their greatness and their worth. The second time he came to him was for the purpose of having certain doubts, which troubled him, cleared up. But when he presented himself before the man of God, he found that at the mere sight of his face, they all vanished as if they had been but a little smoke.

Much more might be told of this wonderful Contemplative; but let what little we have written suffice to lay before pious readers, an example of prayer, to which many aspire, but few attain, because they have neither the courage to persevere, nor the grace to go on knocking till it be given to them. It is, nevertheless, ample enough to show how sluggish and poor we ordinary Christians are, and how far we are from the perfection of the Saints, since this holy man, though so far advanced in sanctity, is not reckoned among those canonized by the Church. What was known of Gregory, little as it was,—and that little manifested sorely against his will,—caused his life to be looked upon as miraculous. For if we re-reflect on the weakness of nature, and consider how reluctant it is to embrace virtue, and how inconstant in its practice, and then turning our eyes to Gregory, observe the heroism of his life, his indomitable perseverance, and his unshaken constancy, we cannot help feeling, that in a certain degree, to have done what he did is very little short of miraculous. This is a conviction which will force itself upon any one who bears in mind that he was a man like ourselves. He had the same feelings, the same affections. Of all these he divested himself. He was poor in spirit, as well as in the literal acceptation of the word. He mortified himself both in mind and in body. He was wonderfully observant of silence, interrupting it only to utter words of wisdom, which had power in them productive of marvellous effects. Totally neglecting and forgetting self, he was ever turned towards God. He entertained the lowest opinion of himself, the highest of others. His confidence in God was unlimited, his dependence on His Divine Providence complete. No idle word was suffered to pass his lips: no slander ever disturbed the serenity of his mind. His soul was flooded with light from the Holy Spirit, by which he had a most intimate and profound knowledge of Holy Scripture. Finally, his union with God was so close, that no circumstance of time, place, or person, ever entirely broke it. All these are, in a certain way, so many miracles wrought by God in His humble servant Gregory, for the instruction and edification of His children. May we profit by the lessons we have learnt from his life, and try, with all our might, to become imbued with the spirit of prayer, if not in the same degree, at least in proportion to that measure of grace, which God will give to all who have good will, and are courageous enough, to aim at a perfect life.

In omnibus glorificetur Deus.

THE END.

PATERNOSTER ROW   *NO. 18, LONDON.*

R. WASHBOURNE'S CATALOGUE.

FEBRUARY, 1876.

The Sufferings of our Lord Jesus Christ. Preached in London by Father Claude de la Colombière, S. J., in the Chapel Royal, St. James's, in the year 1677. 18mo. 1s.; red edges, 1s. 6d.

Lenten Thoughts. Drawn from the Gospel for each day in Lent. By the Bishop of Northampton 1s. 6d.; stronger bound, 2s.; red edges, 2s. 6d.

Devotions for Public and Private Use at the Way of the Cross. By Sister M. F. Clare (the Nun of Kenmare). Illustrated with the Pictures of the Stations. 16mo. 1s.; red edges, 1s. 6d.

The Continental Fish Cook; or, a Few Hints on Maigre Dinners. By M. J. N. de Frederic. 18mo. 1s.

A Treatise on Confidence in the Mercy of God. By Mgr. Languet. Translated by Abbot Burder.

Sanctuary Meditations for Priests and Frequent Communicants. Translated from the Spanish.

Letters to my God-Child—Letter IV. On the Veneration of the Blessed Virgin. By Mrs. Stuart Laidlaw. 16mo. 4d.

Bessy; or the Fatal Consequence of Telling Lies. By the writer of "The Rat Pond, or the Effects of Disobedience." 1s.; cloth gilt, 1s. 6d.

The Serving Boy's Manual and Book of Public Devotions, containing all those prayers and devotions for Sundays and Holidays, usually divided in their recitation between the Priest and the

---

⁎⁎⁎ Though this Catalogue does not contain many of the books of other Publishers, R. W. can supply all of them, no matter by whom they are published.

Congregation. Compiled from approved sources, and adapted to Churches, served either by the Secular or the Regular Clergy.

IN THE PRESS.

Stories for my Children.—The Angels and the Sacraments. Square 16mo. 1s. ; extra cloth, 2s. 6d.

Semi-Tropical Trifles. By Herbert Compton. Fcp. 8vo. Fancy boards, 1s.

Lives of the First Religious of the Visitation of Holy Mary. By Mother Frances Magdalen de Chaugy. With two Photographs. 2 vols., cr. 8vo. 12s.

Easy Way to God. By Cardinal Bona. Translated by Father Collins, author of "Cistercian Legends," "Spiritual Conferences." Fcap. 8vo. 3s.

Legends of the Saints. By M. F. S., author of "Stories of the Saints." Square 16mo.

Spiritual Conferences on the Mysteries of Faith and the Interior Life. By Father Collins, author of "Cistercian Legends," &c. Cr. 8vo. 4s.

Lives of the Saints for every Day in the Year. Translated from M. Didot's edition. Beautifully printed on thick toned paper, with borders from ancient sources, scarlet cloth gilt, gilt edges, 4to. 16s.

The Mass: and a devout method of assisting at it. From the French of M. Tronson. 4d.

Canon Schmid's Tales, selected from his works. New translation, with Original Illustrations, 3s. 6d. Separately: Canary Bird, 6d.; Dove, 6d.; Inundation, 6d. Rose Tree, 6d.; Water Jug, 6d.; Wooden Cross, 6d.

The Elements of Gregorian or Plain Chant and Modern Music. By the Professor of Music and Organist in All Hallows' College, Dublin. 2s. 6d.

The English Religion. Letters addressed to an Irish Gentleman. By A. M. 1s.

Confraternity of the Holy Family. By Henry Edward, Cardinal-Archbishop of Westminster. 8vo. 3d.

Elevations to the Heart of Jesus. By Rev. Father Doyotte, S. J. Fcap. 8vo. 3s.

R. Washbourne, 18 Paternoster Row, London.

S. Vincent Ferrer, of the Order of Friar Preachers: his Life, Spiritual Teaching, and practical Devotion. By the Rev. Fr. Andrew Pradel, of the same Order. Translated from the French by the Rev. Fr. T. A. Dixon, O.P. With a Photograph. Crown 8vo. 5s.

The History of the Italian Revolution. The Revolution of the Barricades. (1796—1849.) By the Chevalier O'Clery, M.P., K.S.G. 8vo. 7s. 6d.

Stories of Holy Lives. By M. F. S., author of "Stories of the Saints," "Catherine Hamilton," "Catherine grown Older," "Tom's Crucifix and other Tales." Fcp. 8vo. 3s.

The Rule of our most holy Father St. Benedict, Patriarch of Monks. From the old English edition of 1638. Edited by one of the Benedictine Fathers of St. Michael's, near Hereford. Fcap. 8vo. 4s. 6d.

First Communion Picture. Tastefully printed in gold and colours. Price 1s., or 10s. a dozen, *net*.

"Just what has long been wanted, a really good picture, with Tablet for First Communion and Confirmation."—*Tablet.*

Book of Family Crests and Mottos. Upwards of four thousand engravings. Eleventh edition. 2 vols., cr. 8vo., 24s.

New Testament, Catholic Vers., Notes and References, 19 large Illustrations. Large 4to., cloth gilt, 12s. 6d.

Road to Heaven. A game for family parties. By Miss M. A. Macdaniel. 3s. 6d.

Balmes' Letters to a Sceptic on Matters of Religion. 6s.

The Dove of the Tabernacle. By Fr. Kinane. 1s. 6d.

Munster Firesides; or, the Barrys of Beigh. By E. Hall. 3s. 6d.

The Mirror of Faith: your Likeness in it. By Father Cuthbert. 3s.

The Christian Instructed in the Nature and Use of Indulgences. By Rev. F. A. Maurel. 3s.

New Model for Youth; or, Life of Richard Aloysius Pennefather. 3s. 6d.

The Blessed Sacrament of the Miracle. 10 Photographs. Price 2s. 6d.

Recollections of Cardinal Wiseman, &c. By M. J. Arnold. 2s. 6d.

R. Washbourne, 18 *Paternoster Row, London.*

The Child. By Mgr. Dupanloup. Translated, 3s. 6d.
The Christian Instructed in the nature and use of Indulgences. By Rev. F. A. Maurel, S.J. 3s.
Protestantism and Liberty. By Professor Ozanam. Translated by W. C. Robinson. 8vo. 1s.
Düsseldorf Society for the Distribution of Good, Religious Pictures. R. Washbourne is now Sole Agent for Great Britain and Ireland. Yearly Subscription is 8s. 6d. *Catalogue post free.*
Düsseldorf Gallery. 8vo. half morocco, 31s. 6d. This volume contains 127 Engravings handsomely bound in half morocco, full gilt. Cash 25s.
Düsseldorf Gallery. 4to. half morocco, £5 5s. This superb work contains 331 Pictures. Handsomely bound in half morocco, full gilt.

"We confidently believe that no wealthy Catholic could possibly see this volume without ordering it for the adornment of his drawing-room table."—*Tablet.* "The most beautiful Catholic gift-book that was ever sent forth from the house of a Catholic publisher."—*Register.*

Catholicism, Liberalism, and Socialism. Translated from the Spanish of Donoso Cortes, by Rev. W. M'Donald. 6s.
The Pope of Rome and the Popes of the Oriental Orthodox Church. By the Rev. Cæsarius Tondini, Barnabite. Second edition. 3s. 6d.

Dramas, Comedies, Farces.

He would be a Lord. From the French of "Le Bourgeois Gentilhomme." Three Acts. (Boys.) 2s.
St. Louis in Chains. Drama in Five Acts, for boys. 2s.
"Well suited for acting in Catholic schools and colleges."—*Tablet.*
The Expiation. A Drama in Three Acts, for boys. 2s.
"Has its scenes laid in the days of the Crusades."—*Register.*
Shandy Maguire. A Farce for boys in Two Acts. 1s.
The Reverse of the Medal. A Drama in Four Acts, for young ladies. 6d.
Ernscliff Hall: or, Two Days Spent with a Great-Aunt. A Drama in Three Acts, for young ladies. 6d.
Filiola. A Drama in Four Acts, for young ladies. 6d.
The Convent Martyr, or Callista. By Dr. Newman. Dramatized by Dr. Husenbeth. 1s.

Garden of the Soul. (WASHBOURNE'S EDITION.) *With Imprimatur of the Archbishop of Westminster.* This edition has over all others the following advantages :—1. Complete order in its arrangements. 2. Introduction of Devotions to Saint Joseph, Patron of the Church. 3. Introduction into the English Devotions for Mass to a very great extent of the Prayers from the Missal. 4. The Full Form of Administration of all the Sacraments publicly administered in Church. 5. The insertion of Indulgences above Indulgenced Prayers. 6. Its large size of type. Embossed, 1s. ; with rims, 1s. 6d. ; with Epistles and Gospels, 1s. 6d. ; with rims, 2s. French morocco, 2s. ; with rims, 2s. 6d. ; with E. and G., 2s. 6d. ; with rims, 3s. French morocco extra gilt, 2s. 6d. ; with rims, 3s. ; with E. and G., 3s. ; with rims, 3s. 6d. Calf or morocco, 4s. ; with rims, 5s. 6d. ; with E. and G., 4s. 6d. ; with rims, 6s. Calf or morocco extra, 5s. ; with rims, 6s. 6d. ; with E. and G., 5s. 6d.; with rims, 7s. Velvet, with rims, 8s., 10s. 6d., and 13s.; with E. and G., 8s. 6d., 11s., and 13s. 6d. Russia, antique, with clasp, 10s. 6d., 12s. 6d.; with E. and G., 11s., 13s. Ivory, 12s. 6d., 16s., 20s., 22s. 6d., and 30s. ; with E. and G., 13s., 16s. 6d., 20s. 6d., 23s. and 30s. 6d. Morocco, with two patent clasps, 12s. Antique bindings, with corners and clasps: morocco, 18s., with E. and G., 18s. 6d. ; russia, 20s., with E. and G., 20s. 6d.

"This is one of the best editions we have seen of one of the best of all our Prayer-books. It is well printed in clear large type, on good paper."—*Catholic Opinion.* "A very complete arrangement of this, which is emphatically the Prayer-book of every Catholic household. It is as cheap as it is good, and we heartily recommend it."—*Universe.* "Two striking features are the admirable order displayed throughout the book, and the insertion of the Indulgences, in small type, above Indulgenced Prayers."—*Weekly Register.*

Some Documents concerning the Association of Prayers, in Honour of Mary Immaculate, for the Return of the Greek-Russian Church to Catholic Unity. By the Rev. C. Tondini. 3d.

R. Washbourne, 18 Paternoster Row, London.

The Epistles and Gospels in cloth, 6d., roan, 1s. 6d.
The Little Garden. Cloth, 6d., with rims, 1s.; embossed, 9d., with rims, 1s. 3d.; roan, 1s., with rims, 1s. 6d.; french morocco, 1s. 6d., with rims, 2s.; french morocco, extra gilt, 2s., with rims, 2s. 6d.; imitation ivory, with rims, 3s.; calf or morocco, 3s., with rims, 4s.; calf or morocco, extra gilt, 4s., with rims, 5s.; velvet, with rims, 5s., 8s. 6d., 10s. 6d.; russia, with clasp, 8s.; ivory, with rims, 10s. 6d., 13s., 15s., 17s. 6d.; antique binding, with clasps: morocco, 16s.; russia, 17s. 6d; morocco, with a patent clasp, 10s. 6d.; with oxydized silver or gilt mountings, in morocco case, 25s.

A Few Words from Lady Mildred's Housekeeper. 2d.
"If any of our lady readers wish to give to their servants some hints as to the necessity of laying up some part of their wages instead of spending their money in dressing above their station, let them get 'A Few Words from Lady Mildred's Housekeeper,' and present it for the use of the servants' hall or downstairs departments. The good advice of an experienced upper servant on such subjects ought not to fall on unwilling ears."—*Register.*

Religious Reading.

"Vitis Mystica;" or, the True Vine. A Treatise on the Passion of Our Lord. Translated, with Preface, by the Rev. W. R. Bernard Brownlow. With Frontispiece. 18mo. 4s., red edges, 4s. 6d.
"It is a pity that such a beautiful treatise should for so many centuries have remained untranslated into our tongue."—*Tablet.* "It will be found very acceptable spiritual food."—*Church Herald.* "We heartily recommend it for its unction and deep sense of the beauties of nature."—*The Month.* "Full of deep spiritual lore."—*Register.* "Every chapter of this little volume affords abundant matter for meditation."—*Universe.* "An excellent translation of a beautiful treatise."—*Dublin Review.*

Ebba; or, the Supernatural Power of the Blessed Sacrament. In French. 12mo. 1s. 6d.; cloth gilt, 2s. 6d.
"There are thoughts in the work which we value highly."—*Dublin Review.* "Will do good to all who read it."—*Universe.*

Apostleship of Prayer. By Rev. H. Ramière. 6s.

The Happiness of Heaven. By a Father of the Society of Jesus. Fcap. 8vo. 4s.

God our Father. By the same Author. Fcap. 8vo. 4s.

Holy Places; their Sanctity and Authenticity. By the Rev. Fr. Philpin. With Maps. Crown 8vo. 6s.

"It displays an amount of patient research not often to be met with."—*Universe.* ", Dean Stanley and other sinners in controversy are treated with great gentleness. They are indeed thoroughly exposed and refuted."—*Register.* "Fr. Philpin has a particularly nervous and fresh style of handling his subject, with an occasional picturesqueness of epithet or simile."—*Tablet.* "We do not question his learning and industry, and yet we cannot think them to have been uselessly expended on this work."—*Spectator.* ". . . Fr. Philpin there weighs the comparative value of extraordinary, ordinary, and natural evidence, and gives an admirable summary of the witness of the early centuries regarding the holy places of Jerusalem, with archæological and architectural proofs. It is a complete treatise of the subject."—*The Month.* "The author treats his subject with a thorough system, and a competent knowledge. It is a book of singular attractiveness and considerable merit."—*Church Herald.* "Fr. Philpin's very interesting book appears most opportunely, and at a time when pilgrimages have been revived."—*Dublin Review.*

The Consoler; or, Pious Readings addressed to the Sick and to all who are afflicted. By the Rev. P. J. Lambilotte, S.J. Translated by the Right Rev. Abbot Burder, O. Cist. Fcp. 8vo. 4s. 6d., red edges, 5s.

"As 'The Consoler' has the merit of being written in plain and simple language, and while deeply spiritual contains no higher flights into the regions of mysticism where poor and ignorant readers would be unable to follow, it is very specially adapted for one of the subjects which its writer had in view, namely, its introduction into hospitals."—*Tablet.* "A work replete with wise comfort for every affliction."—*Universe.* "A spiritual treatise of great beauty and value."—*Church Herald.*

The Selva, or a Collection of Matter for Sermons. By St. Liguori. 5s.

The Souls in Purgatory. Translated from the French, by the Right Rev. Abbot Burder, O. Cist. 32mo. 3d.

"It will be found most useful as an aid to the cultivation of this especial devotion."—*Register.*

Flowers of Christian Wisdom. By Lucien Henry. With a Preface by the Right Hon. Lady Herbert of Lea. 18mo. 2s.; red edges, 2s. 6d.

"A compilation of some of the most beautiful thoughts and passages in the works of the Fathers, the great schoolmen, and eminent modern Churchmen, and will probably secure a good circulation."—*Church Times.* "It is a compilation of gems of thought, carefully selected."—*Tablet.* "It is a small but exquisite bouquet, like that which S. Francis of Sales has prepared for *Philothea.*"—*Universe.*

A General History of the Catholic Church: from the commencement of the Christian Era until the present time. By the Abbé Darras. 4 vols., large 8vo. cloth, 48s.

The Book of Perpetual Adoration; or, the Love of Jesus in the most Holy Sacrament of the Altar. By Mgr. Boudon. Edited by the Rev. J. Redman, D.D. Fcap. 8vo. 3s.; red edges, 3s. 6d.

"This new translation is one of Boudon's most beautiful works, ... and merits that welcome in no ordinary degree."—*Tablet*. "The devotions at the end will be very acceptable aids in visiting the Blessed Sacrament, and there are two excellent methods for assisting at Mass."—*The Month*. "It has been pronounced by a learned and pious French priest to be 'the most beautiful of all books written in honour of the Blessed Sacrament.'"—*The Nation*.

Spiritual Works of Louis of Blois, Abbot of Liesse. Edited by the Rev. John Edward Bowden, of the Oratory. Fcap. 8vo. 3s. 6d; red edges, 4s.

"No more important or welcome addition could have been made to our English ascetical literature than this little book. It is a model of good translation."—*Dublin Review*. "This handy little volume will certainly become a favourite."—*Tablet*. "Elegant and flowing."—*Register*. "Most useful of meditations."—*Catholic Opinion*.

Heaven Opened by the Practice of Frequent Confession and Communion. By the Abbé Favre. Translated from the French, carefully revised by a Father of the Society of Jesus. Third Edition. Fcap. 8vo. 3s. 6d.; red edges, 4s. Cheap edit. 2s.

"This beautiful little book of devotion. We may recommend it to the clergy as well as to the laity."—*Tablet*. "It is filled with quotations from the Holy Scriptures, the Fathers, and the Councils of the Church, and thus will be found of material assistance to the clergy, as a storehouse of doctrinal and ascetical authorities on the two great sacraments of Holy Eucharist and Penance."—*Register*.

The Spiritual Life.—Conferences delivered to the *Enfants de Marie* by Père Ravignan. Cr. 8vo. 5s.

"Père Ravignan's words are as applicable to the ladies of London as to those of Paris. They could not have a better book for their spiritual reading."—*Tablet*. "A depth of eloquence and power of exhortation which few living preachers can rival."—*Church Review*.

The Supernatural Life. Translated from the French of Mgr. Mermillod, with a Preface by Lady Herbert. Cr. 8vo. 5s.

Holy Communion: it is my Life. By H. Lebon. 4s.

R. Washbourne, 18 Paternoster Row, London.

The Eucharist and the Christian Life. By Mgr. de la
   Bouillerie. Translated. Fcap. 8vo. 3s. 6d.
The Jesuits, and other Essays. By Willis Nevin.
   Fcap. 8vo. 2s. 6d.
On Contemporary Prophecies. By Mgr. Dupanloup.
   Translated by Rev. Dr. Redmond. 8vo. 1s.
Good Thoughts for Priests and People; or Short
   Meditations for Every Day in the Year. By Rev.
   T. Noethen. 12mo. 8s.
One Hundred Pious Reflections. Extracted from
   Alban Butler's "Lives of the Saints." 18mo.
   cloth, red edges, 2s.; cheap edition, 1s.

"A happy idea. The author of 'The Lives of the Saints' had a way of breathing into his language the unction and force which carries the truth of the Gospel into the heart."—*Letter to the Editor from* THE RIGHT REV. DR. ULLATHORNE, BISHOP OF BIRMINGHAM. "Well selected, sufficiently short, and printed in good bold type."—*Tablet.* "Good, sound, practical."—*Church Herald.*

The Imitation of Christ. With reflections. 32mo.
   1s. Persian calf, 3s. 6d. Also an Edition with
   ornamental borders. Fcap. cloth, red edges, 3s. 6d.
Following of Christ. Small pocket edition, 1s. cloth;
   1s. 6d. embossed; roan, 2s.; French morocco, 2s.
   6d.; calf or morocco, 4s. 6d.; calf or morocco
   extra gilt, 5s. 6d.; ivory, 15s. and 16s.; morocco,
   antique, 17s. 6d.; russia antique, 20s.
Conversion of the Teutonic Race. By Mrs. Hope,
   author of "Early Martyrs." Edited by the Rev.
   Father Dalgairns. 2 vols. crown 8vo. 12s.
   I. Conversion of the Franks and the English, 6s.
   II. S. Boniface and the Conversion of Germany, 6s.

"It is good in itself, possessing considerable literary merit; it forms one of the few Catholic books brought out in this country which are not translations or adaptations."—*Dublin Review.* "It is a great thing to find a writer of a book of this class so clearly grasping, and so boldly setting forth, truths which, familiar as they are to scholars, are still utterly unknown by most of the writers of our smaller literature."—*Saturday Review.* "A very valuable work . . . . Mrs. Hope has compiled an original history, which gives constant evidence of great erudition, and sound historical judgment."—*Month.* "This is a most taking book: it is solid history and romance in one."—*Catholic Opinion.* "It is carefully, and in many parts beautifully written."—*Universe.*

R. Washbourne, 18 Paternoster Row, London.

Contemplations on the Most Holy Sacrament of the Altar, drawn from the Sacred Scriptures. 18mo. cloth, 2s.; cloth extra, red edges, 2s. 6d.

"This is a welcome addition to our books of Scriptural devotion. It contains thirty-four excellent subjects of reflection before the Blessed Sacrament, or for making a spiritual visit to the Blessed Sacrament at home; for the use of the sick."—*Dublin Review.*

Cistercian Order: its Mission and Spirit. Comprising the Life of S. Robert of Newminster, and the Life of S. Robert of Knaresborough. By the author of "Cistercian Legends." Crown 8vo. 3s. 6d.

Cistercian Legends of the 13th Century. Translated from the Latin by the Rev. Henry Collins. 3s.

"Interesting records of Cistercian sanctity and cloistral experience."—*Dublin Review.* "A casquet of jewels."—*Weekly Register.* "Most beautiful legends, full of deep spiritual reading."—*Tablet.* "Well translated, and beautifully got up."—*Month.* "A compilation of anecdotes, full of heavenly wisdom."—*Catholic Opinion.*

The Directorium Asceticum; or Guide to the Spiritual Life. By Scaramelli. Translated and edited at St. Beuno's College. 4 vols. crown 8vo. 24s.

Maxims of the Kingdom of Heaven. New and enlarged Edition. 5s.; red edges, 5s. 6d.; calf or morocco, 10s. 6d.

"The selections on every subject are numerous, and the order and arrangement of the chapters will greatly facilitate meditation and reference."—*Freeman's Journal.* "We are glad to see that this admirable devotional work, of which we have before spoken in warm praise, has reached a second issue."—*Weekly Register.* "It has an Introduction by J. H. N., and bears the Imprimatur of the Archbishop of Westminster. We need say no more in its praise."—*Tablet.* "A most beautiful little book."—*Catholic Opinion.* "This priceless volume."—*Universe.* "Most suitable for meditation and reference."—*Dublin Review.*

The Oxford Undergraduate of Twenty Years Ago: his Religion, his Studies, his Antics. By a Bachelor of Arts. [Author of "The Comedy of Convocation."] 2s. 6d.; cloth, 3s. 6d.

"The writing is full of brilliancy and point."—*Tablet.* "Time has not dimmed the author's recollection, and has no doubt served to sharpen his sense of undergraduate humour and his reading of undergraduate character."—*Examiner.* "It will deservedly attract attention, not only by the briskness and liveliness of its style, but also by the accuracy of the picture which it probably gives of an individual experience."—*The Month.*

R. Washbourne, 18 Paternoster Row, London.

The Infallibility of the Pope. A Lecture. By the Author of "The Oxford Undergraduate." 8vo. 1s.

"A splendid lecture, by one who thoroughly understands his subject, and in addition is possessed of a rare power of language in which to put before others what he himself knows so well."—*Universe*. "There are few writers so well able to make things plain and intelligible as the author of 'The Comedy of Convocation.'... The lecture is a model of argument and style."—*Register*.

Comedy of Convocation in the English Church. Edited by Archdeacon Chasuble, D.D. 2s. 6d.

Reply to the Bishop of Ripon's Attack on the Catholic Church. By the same Author. 6d.

The Harmony of Anglicanism. Report of a Conference on Church Defence. [By T. W. M. Marshall, Esq.] 8vo. 2s. 6d.

"'Church Defence' is characterized by the same caustic irony, the same good-natured satire, the same logical acuteness which distinguished its predecessor, the 'Comedy of Convocation.'... A more scathing bit of irony we have seldom met with."—*Tablet*.

"Clever, humorous, witty, learned, written by a keen but sarcastic observer of the Establishment, it is calculated to make defenders wince as much as it is to make all others smile."—*Nonconformist*.

Thy Gods, O Israel. A Picture in Verse of the Religious Anomalies of our Time. Cr. 8vo. 2s.

The Roman Question. By Dr. Husenbeth. 6d.

Consoling Thoughts of St. Francis de Sales. By Père Huguet. 18mo., 2s.

Holy Readings. Short Selections from well-known Authors. By J. R. Digby Beste, Esq. 32mo. cloth, 2s.; cloth, red edges, 2s. 6d.; roan, 3s.; morocco, 6s. [See "Catholic Hours," p. 23.]

St. Peter; his Name and his Office as set forth in Holy Scripture. By T. W. Allies. *Second Edition.* Revised. Crown 8vo. 5s.

"A standard work. There is no single book in English, on the Catholic side, which contains the Scriptural argument about St. Peter and the Papacy so clearly or conclusively put."—*Month*.
"An admirable volume."—*The Universe*. "This valuable work."—*Weekly Register*. "A second edition, with a new and very touching preface."—*Dublin Review*.

Sancti Alphonsi Doctoris Officium Parvum—Novena and Little Office in honour of St. Alphonsus. Fcap. 8vo. 1s.; cloth, 2s.; cloth extra, 3s.

The Life of Pleasure. Translated from the French of Mgr. Dechamps. Fcap. 8vo. 1s. 6d.
Sure Way to Heaven: a little Manual for Confession and Holy Communion. 32mo. cloth, 6d. Persian 2s. 6d. Calf or morocco, 3s. 6d.
Compendium of the History of the Catholic Church. By Rev. T. Noethen. 12mo. 8s.
History of the Catholic Church, for schools. By Rev. T. Noethen. 12mo. 5s. 6d.
Benedictine Almanack. Price 2d.
Catholic Calendar and Church Guide. Price 6d.; interleaved, 8d.
Catholic Directory for Scotland. 1s.
Dr. Pusey's Eirenicon considered in Relation to Catholic Unity. By H. N. Oxenham. 2s. 6d.
Familiar Instructions on Christian Truths. By a Priest. No. 1, Detraction. 4d. No. 2, The Dignity of the Priesthood. 3d. No. 3, Necessity of hearing the Word of God. Why it produces no fruit, and how to be heard. On the necessity of Faith. 3d.
Sweetness of Holy Living; or Honey culled from the Flower Garden of S. Francis of Sales. 1s. French morocco, 3s.
" In it will be found some excellent aids to devotion and meditation."—*Weekly Register.*
The Tradition of the Syriac Church of Antioch, concerning the Primacy and Prerogatives of S. Peter, and of his successors, the Roman Pontiffs. By the Most Rev. C. B. Benni. 8vo. 21s., for 7s. 6d.
Père Lacordaire's Conferences. God, 6s. Jesus Christ, 6s. God and Man, 6s. Life, 6s.
Commonitory of S. Vincent of Lerins. 12mo. 1s. 3d.
Men and Women of the English Reformation, from the days of Wolsey to the death of Cranmer. By S. H. Burke, M.A. Vol. i. is out of print. Vol. ii., 6s. 6d.
 The chief topics of importance in the second volume are: Archbishop Cranmer's opinions upon Confession; The Religious Houses of Olden England; Burnet as a Historian; What were Lord Cromwell's Religious Sentiments? Effects of the Confiscation on the

People ; The Church and the Holy Scriptures ; Death-bed Horrors of Henry VIII.; Scenes upon the Scaffold—Lady Jane Grey's heroic Death ; The Rack and the Stake ; The Archbishop condemned to be Burnt Alive—Awful Scene ; A General View of Cranmer's Life.

" It contains a great amount of curious and useful information."—*Dublin Review.* "Interesting and valuable."—*Tablet.* "The only dispassionate record of a much contested epoch we have ever read."—*Cosmopolitan.* "So forcibly, but truthfully written, that it should be in the hands of every seeker after truth."—*Catholic Opinion.*—"On all hands admitted to be one of the most valuable historical works ever published."—*Nation.* "Full of interest."—*Church Review.* "Replete with information."—*Church Times.*

A Devout Paraphrase on the Seven Penitential Psalms ; or, a Practical Guide to Repentance. By the Rev. Fr. Blyth. To which is added :—Necessity of Purifying the Soul, by St. Francis of Sales. 18mo., 1s. 6d. ; red edges, 2s. ; cheap edition, 1s.

"A new edition of a book well known to our grandfathers. The work is full of devotion and of the spirit of prayer."—*Universe.* "A very excellent work, and ought to be in the hands of every Catholic."—*Waterford News.*

A New Miracle at Rome ; through the Intercession of Blessed John Berchmans. 2d.

Cure of Blindness ; through the Intercession of Our Lady and St. Ignatius. 2d.

BY THE POOR CLARES OF KENMARE.

Woman's Work in Modern Society. 7s. 6d.
A Nun's Advice to her Girls. 2s. 6d.
Daily Steps to Heaven. Fcap. 8vo. 4s. 6d.
Book of the Blessed Ones. 4s. 6d.
Jesus and Jerusalem ; or, the Way Home. 4s. 6d.

A Homely Discourse ; Mary Magdalen. Cr. 8vo. 6d.
Extemporaneous Speaking. By Rev. T. J. Potter. 5s.
Pastor and People. By Rev. T. J. Potter. 6s.
Eight Short Sermon Essays. By Dr. Redmond. 1s.
One Hundred Short Sermons. By Rev. H. T. Thomas. 8vo. 12s.
Catholic Sermons. By Father Burke, and others. 2s.
The Light of the Holy Spirit in the World. Five Sermons by the Rt. Rev. Bishop Hedley, O.S.B. 1s. ; cloth, 1s. 6d.

R. Washbourne, 18 *Paternoster Row, London.*

The Church of England and its Defenders. By the Rev. W. R. Bernard Brownlow. 8vo. 1s. 6d.
Lectures on the Life, Writings, and Times of Edmund Burke. By Professor Robertson. 3s. 6d.
Professor Robertson's Lectures on Modern History and Biography. Crown 8vo. cloth, 6s.
The Knight of the Faith. By the Rev. Dr. Laing.
1. A Favourite Fallacy about Private Judgment. 1d.
2. Catholic not Roman Catholic. 4d.
3. Rationale of the Mass. 1s.
4. Challenge to the Churches of England, Scotland, and all Protestant Denominations. 1d.
5. Absurd Protestant Opinions concerning *Intention*, and Spelling Book of Christian Philosophy. 4d.
6. Whence the Monarch's right to rule. 2s. 6d.
7. Protestantism against the Natural Moral Law. 1d.
8. What is Christianity? 6d.
Abridged Explanation of the Medal or Cross of S. Benedict. 1d.
Diary of a Confessor of the Faith. 12mo. 1s.
Sursum, 1s. Homeward, 2s. Both by Rev. Fr. Rawes.
Sermon at the Month's Mind of the Most Rev. Dr. Spalding, Archbishop of Baltimore. 1s.
Exposition of the Epistles of St. Paul. By the Right Rev. Dr. MacEvilly. 2 vols. 18s.
Commentary on the Psalms. By Bellarmin. 4to. 6s.
Monastic Legends. By E. G. K. Browne. 8vo. 6d.

BY DR. MANNING, ARCHBISHOP OF WESTMINSTER.

The Convocation in Crown and Council. 6d. net.
Confidence in God. Reprinting.
Temporal Sovereignty of the Popes. 1s.; cloth, 1s. 6d.
The Church, the Spirit, and the Word. 6d.

BY THE PASSIONIST FATHERS.

The School of Jesus Crucified. Reprinting.
The Manual of the Cross and Passion. 32mo. 2s. 6d.
The Manual of the Seven Dolours. 32mo. 1s. 6d.
The Christian Armed. 32mo. 1s. 6d.; mor. 3s. 6d.
Guide to Sacred Eloquence. 2s.

Religious Instruction.

The Catechism, Illustrated with Passages from the Holy Scriptures. Arranged by the Rev. J. B. Bagshawe, with Imprimatur. Crown 8vo. 2s. 6d.

"I believe the Catechism to be one of the best possible books of controversy, to those, at least, who are inquiring with a real desire to find the truth."—*Extract from the Preface.*
"An excellent idea. The very thing of all others that is needed by many under instruction."—*Tablet.* "It is a book which will do incalculable good. Our priests will hail with pleasure so valuable a help to their weekly instructions in the Catechism, while in schools its value will be equally recognized."—*Weekly Register.*
"A work of great merit."—*Church Herald.* "We can hardly wish for anything better, either in intention or in performance."—*The Month.* "Very valuable."—*Dublin Review.*

The Threshold of the Catholic Church. A course of Plain Instructions for those entering her Communion. By Rev. J. B. Bagshawe. Cr. 8vo. 4s.

"A scholarly, well-written book, full of information."—*Church Herald.* "An admirable book, which will be of infinite service to thousands."—*Universe.* "Plain, practical, and unpretentious, it exhausts so entirely the various subjects of instruction necessary for our converts, that few missionary priests will care to dispense with its assistance."—*Register.* "It has very special merits of its own. . It is the work, not only of a thoughtful writer and good theologian, but of a wise and experienced priest."—*Dublin Review.* "Its characteristic is the singular simplicity and clearness with which everything is explained. . . It will save priests hours and days of time."—*Tablet.* "There is much in it with which we thoroughly agree."—*Church Times.* "There was a great want of a manual of instruction for convents, and the want has now been supplied, and in the most satisfactory manner."—*The Month.*

The Catechism of Christian Doctrine. Approved for the use of the Faithful in all the Dioceses of England and Wales. Price 1d.; cloth, 2d.

A First Sequel to the Catechism. By the Rev. J. Nary. 32mo. 1d.

"It will recommend itself to teachers in Catholic schools as one peculiarly adapted to the use of such children as have mastered the Catechism, and yet have nothing else to fall back upon for higher religious instruction."—*Weekly Register.*

Catechism made Easy. A Familiar Explanation of "The Catechism of Christian Doctrine." By Rev. H. Gibson. Vol. I., 4s. Vol. II., 4s.

A General Catechism of the Christian Doctrine. By the Right Rev. Dr. Poirier. 18mo. 9d.

A Dogmatic Catechism. By Frassinetti. Translated from the original Italian by the Oblate Fathers of St. Charles. Fcap. 8vo. 3s.

"We give a few extracts from Frassinetti's work, as samples of its excellent execution."—*Dublin Review.* "Needs no commendation."—*Month.* "It will be found useful, not only to catechists, but also for the instruction of converts from the middle class of society."—*Tablet.*

Mgr. de Ségur's Books for Little Children. Translated. Confession; Holy Communion; Child Jesus; Piety; Prayer; Temptation. 3d. each.

The Seven Sacraments explained and defended. Edited by a Catholic Clergyman. 1s. 6d.

Burton's Ecclesiastical History. 1s.

Protestant Principles Examined by the Written Word. Originally entitled, "The Protestant's Trial by the Written Word." *New edition.* 18mo. 1s.

"An excellent book."—*Church News.* "A good specimen of the concise controversial writing of English Catholics in the early part of the seventeenth century."—*Catholic Opinion.* "A little book which might be consulted profitably by any Catholic."—*Church Times.* "A clever little manual."—*Westminster Gazette.* "A useful little volume."—*The Month.* "An excellent little book."—*Weekly Register.* "A well-written and well-argued treatise."—*Tablet.*

Descriptive Guide to the Mass. By the Rev. Dr. Laing. 1s.; extra cloth, 1s. 6d.

"An attempt to exhibit the structure of the Mass. The logical relation of parts is ingeniously effected by an elaborate employment of differences of type, so that the classification, down to the minutest subdivision, may at once be caught by the eye."—*Tablet.*

The Necessity of Enquiry as to Religion. By Henry John Pye, M.A. 4d.; cloth, 6d.

"Mr. Pye is particularly plain and straightforward."—*Tablet.* "It is calculated to do much good. We recommend it to the clergy, and think it a most useful work to place in the hands of all who are under instruction."—*Westminster Gazette.* "A thoroughly searching little pamphlet."—*Universe.* "A clever little pamphlet. Each point is treated briefly and clearly."—*Catholic Opinion.*

The Grounds of Catholic Doctrine. By Dr. Challoner. Large type edition. 18mo. cloth, 4d.

Dr. Butler's *First* Catechism, ½d. *Second* Catechism, 1d.; *Third* Catechism, 1½d.

Dr. Doyle's Catechism, 1½d.

Lessons on the Christian Doctrine, 1½d.

R. Washbourne, 18 Paternoster Row, London.

Fleury's Historical Catechism. Large edition, 1½d.
Bible History for the use of Catholic Schools and Families. By the Rev. R. Gilmour. 2s.
Origin and Progress of Religious Orders, and Happiness of a Religious State. By Fr. Jerome Platus, S.J.; translated by Patrick Mannock. 2s. 6d.
"The whole work is evidently calculated to impress any reader with the great advantages attached to a religious life."—*Register.*
Children of Mary in the World. 32mo. 1d.
The Christian Teacher. By Ven. de la Salle. 1s. 8d.
Christian Politeness. By the Ven. de la Salle. 1s.
Duties of a Christian. By the Ven. de la Salle. 2s.
The Young Catholic's Guide to Confession and Holy Communion. By Dr. Kenny. *Third edition.* Paper, 4d.; cloth, 6d.; cloth, red edges, 9d.
Instructions for the Sacrament of Confirmation. 6d.
Auricular Confession. By Rev. Dr. Melia. 1s. 6d.
Explanation of the Epistles and Gospels, &c. By the Rev. Fr. Goffine. Illustrated. 7s.
Rules for a Christian Life. By S. Charles Borromeo. 2d.
Anglican Orders. By the Very Rev. Canon Williams. *Second Edition.* Crown 8vo. 3s. 6d.
Little by Little; or, the Penny Bank. By the Rev. Fr. Richardson. 1d.
The Crusade, or Catholic Association for the Suppression of Drunkenness. By the same. 1d.
Catholic Sick and Benefit Club; or, the Guild of our Lady, and St. Joseph's Burial Society. By the Rev. Fr. Richardson. 32mo. 4d. Burial Society by itself, 2d.
Home Rule. By Rev. Fr. Richardson. 1d.
The Monks of Iona and the Duke of Argyll. By the Rev. J. Stewart M'Corry, D.D. 8vo. 3s. 6d.

Lives of Saints, &c.

Life of the Ven. Anna Maria Taigi. Translated from the French of Calixte, by A. V. Smith Sligo. 8vo. 5s.
Butler's Lives of the Saints. 2 vols., 8vo., cloth, 28s.; or in cloth gilt, 34s.; or in 4 vols., 8vo., cloth, 32s.; or in cloth gilt, 48s.; or in leather gilt, 64s.

R. Washbourne, 18 *Paternoster Row, London.*

Life, Passion, Death, and Resurrection of Our Blessed Lord. Translated from Ribadeneira. 1s.

Oratorian Lives of the Saints. Second Series. Post 8vo.
Vol. I.—S. Bernardine of Siena. 5s.
Vol. II.—S. Philip Benizi. 5s.
Vol. III.—S. Veronica Giuliani, and Blessed Battista Varani. 5s.
Vol. IV.—S. John of God. 5s.

The works translated from will be in most cases the Lives drawn up *for* or *from* the processes of canonization or beatification, as being more full, more authentic, and more replete with anecdote, thus enabling the reader to become better acquainted with the Saint's disposition and spirit; while the simple matter-of-fact style of the narrative is, from its unobtrusive character, more adapted for spiritual reading than the views and generalizations, and prologetic extenuations of more recent biographers. The work is published with the permission and approval of superiors. Every volume containing the Life of a person not yet canonized or beatified by the Church will be prefaced by a protest in conformity with the decree of Urban VIII., and in all Lives which introduce questions of mystical theology great care will be taken to publish nothing which has not had adequate sanction, or without the reader being informed of the nature and amount of the sanction. Each volume is embellished with a Portrait of the Saint.

Life of Sister Mary Cherubina Clare of S. Francis, Translated from the Italian, with Preface by Lady Herbert. Cr. 8vo. with Photograph, 3s. 6d.

Stories of the Saints. By M. F. S., author of "Tom's Crucifix, and other Tales," "Catherine Hamilton," &c. 2 vols., each 3s. 6d., gilt, 4s. 6d.

Life of B. Giovanni Colombini. By Feo Belcari. Translated from the editions of 1541 and 1832. with a Photograph. Cr. 8vo. 3s. 6d.

Sketch of the Life and Letters of the Countess Adelstan. By E. A. M., author of "Rosalie, or the Memoirs of a French Child," "Life of Paul Seigneret, &c." 2s. 6d.

Life and Prophecies of S. Columbkille, 3s. 6d.

LIVES OF THE ENGLISH SAINTS.

Life of St. Augustine of Canterbury. 12mo. 3s. 6d.
Life of St. German. 12mo. cloth, 3s. 6d.
Life of Stephen Langton. 12mo. cloth, 2s. 6d.

Prince and Saviour. A Life of Christ for the Young. By Rosa Mulholland. 6d. Enlarged edition with extra matter. With 12 beautiful illustrations in gold and colours. Fcap. 8vo. 2s. 6d.

S. Paul of the Cross. By the Passionist Fathers. 2s. 6d.

Nano Nagle. By Rev. W. Hutch, D.D. 7s. 6d.

Life of St. Boniface, and the Conversion of Germany. By Mrs. Hope. Edited, with a Preface, by the Rev. Father Dalgairns. Cr. 8vo. 6s.

"Every one knows the story of S. Boniface's martyrdom, but every one has not heard it so stirringly set forth as in her 22nd chapter by Mrs. Hope."—*Dublin Review.*

Louise Lateau: her Life, Stigmata, and Ecstasies. By Dr. Lefebvre. Translated from the French by T. S. Shepard. Fcap. 8vo. 2s.

Venerable Mary Christina of Savoy. 6d.

Memoirs of a Guardian Angel. Fcap. 8vo. 4s.

Life of St. Patrick. 12mo. 1s.

Life of St. Bridget, and of other Saints of Ireland. 1s.

Insula Sanctorum: the Island of Saints. 1s.; cloth, 2s.

Life of Paul Seigneret, Seminarist of Saint-Sulpice. Fcap. 8vo., 1s.; cloth extra, 1s. 6d.; gilt, 2s.

"An affecting and well-told narrative... It will be a great favourite, especially with our pure-minded, high-spirited young people." —*Universe.* "Paul Seigneret was remarkable for the simplicity and the heroism of both his natural and his religious character."—*Tablet.* "We commend it to parents with sons under their care, and especially do we recommend it to those who are charged with the education and training of our Catholic youth."—*Register.*

A Daughter of St. Dominic. By Grace Ramsay. Fcap. 8vo. 1s. 6d.; cloth extra, 2s.

"A beautiful little work. The narrative is highly interesting."— *Dublin Review.* "It is full of courage and faith and Catholic heroism."—*Universe.* "One who has lived and died in our own day, who led the common life of every one else, but yet who learned how to supernaturalize this life in so extraordinary a way that we forget 'the doctor's daughter in a provincial town,' while reading Grace Ramsay's beautiful picture of the wonders effected by her ubiquitous charity, and still more by her fervent prayer."—*Tablet.*

The Glory of St. Vincent de Paul. By the Most Rev. Dr. Manning, Archbishop of Westminster. 1s.

Life of S. Edmund of Canterbury. From the French of the Rev. Father Massé, S. J. 1s. and 1s. 6d.

The Life of St. Francis of Assisi. Translated from the Italian of St. Bonaventure by Miss Lockhart. With a Preface by His Grace the Archbishop of Westminster. Fcap. 8vo. 4s. gilt.
Life of Fr. de Ravignan. Crown 8vo. 9s.
The Pilgrimage to Paray le Monial, with a brief notice of the Blessed Margaret Mary. 6d.
Patron Saints. By Eliza Allen Starr. Cr. 8vo. 10s.
His Eminence Cardinal Wiseman ; with full account of his Obsequies ; Funeral Oration by Archbishop Manning, &c. 1s. ; cloth, red edges, 1s. 6d.
Count de Montalembert. By George White. 6d.
Life of Mgr. Weedall. By Dr. Husenbeth. 7s. 6d., for 1s.
Life of Pope Pius IX. 6d. Cheap edition, 1d.
Challoner's Memoirs of Missionary Priests. 8vo. 6s.

BY THE POOR CLARES OF KENMARE.

O'Connell : his Life and Times. 2 vols., 24s.
The Liberator : his Public Speeches and Letters. 2 vols., 24s.
Life of Father Matthew. 2s. 6d.
Life of St. Aloysius. 6d. ; St. Joseph, 6d., cloth, 9d. ; St. Patrick, 6d., cloth, 9d.
Life of St. Patrick. Illustrated by Doyle. 4to. 20s.

Our Lady.

Regina Sæculorum, or, Mary venerated in all Ages. Devotions to the Blessed Virgin from ancient sources. Fcap. 8vo. 3s.
Readings for the Feasts of Our Lady, and especially for the Month of May. By the Rev. A. P. Bethell. 18mo. 1s. 6d. ; cheap edition, 1s.
The History of the Blessed Virgin. By the Abbé Orsini. Translated from the French by the Very Rev. F. C. Husenbeth, D.D. With eight Illustrations. Crown 8vo. 3s. 6d.
Manual of Devotions in Honour of Our Lady of Sorrows. Compiled by the Clergy at St. Patrick's Soho. 18mo. 1s. ; cloth, red edges, 1s. 6d.

Our Blessed Lady of Lourdes: a Faithful Narrative of the Apparitions of the Blessed Virgin. By F. C. Husenbeth, D.D. 18mo. 6d.; cloth, 1s.; with Novena, 1s.; cloth, 1s. 6d. Novena, separately, 4d.; Litany, 1d., or 6s. per 100.

Devotion to Our Lady in North America. By the Rev. Xavier Donald Macleod. 8vo. 7s. 6d.

"The work of an author than whom few more gifted writers have ever appeared among us. It is not merely a religious work, but it has all the charms of an entertaining book of travels. We can hardly find words to express our high admiration of it."—*Weekly Register*.

Life of the Ever-Blessed Virgin. Proposed as a Model to Christian Women. 1s.

The Blessed Virgin's Root traced in the Tribe of Ephraim. By the Rev. Dr. Laing. 8vo. 10s. 6d.

Litany of the Seven Dolours. 1d. each, or 6s. per 100.

Month of Mary for all the Faithful. By Rev. P. Comerford. 1s.

Month of Mary for Interior Souls. By M. A. Macdaniel. 18mo. 2s.

Month of Mary, principally for the use of religious communities. 18mo. 1s. 6d.

A Devout Exercise in Honour of the Blessed Virgin Mary. From the Psalter and Prayers of S. Bonaventure. In Latin and English, with Indulgences applicable to the Holy Souls. 32mo. 1s.

The Definition of the Immaculate Conception. 6d.

The Little Office of the Immaculate Conception. In Latin and English. By the Very Rev. Dr. Husenbeth. 32mo. 4d.; cloth, 6d.; roan, 1s.; calf or morocco, 2s. 6d.

Life of Our Lady in Verse. Edited by C. E. Tame. 2s.

Our Lady's Lament, and the Lamentation of St. Mary Magdalene. Edited by C. E. Tame. 2s.

The Virgin Mary. By Dr. Melia. 8vo. 11s. 3d. cash.

Archconfraternity of Our Lady of Angels. 1s. per 100.

Litany of Our Lady of Angels. 1s. per 100.

Concise Portrait of the Blessed Virgin. 1s. per 100.

Origin of the Blue Scapular. 1d.

Miraculous Prayer—August Queen of Angels. 1s. 100.

Prayer-Books.

Washbourne's Edition of the "Garden of the Soul," in medium-sized type (small type as a rule being avoided). For prices see page 5.

The Little Garden. 6d., and upwards. *See page* 6.

The Lily of St. Joseph; a little Manual of Prayers and Hymns for Mass. Price 2d.; cloth, 3d.; or with gilt lettering, 4d.; more strongly bound, 6d.; or with gilt edges, 8d.; roan, 1s.; French morocco, 1s. 6d.; calf, or morocco, 2s.; gilt, 2s. 6d.

¶ ["It supplies a want which has long been felt; a prayer-book for children, which is not a childish book, a handy book for boys and girls, and for men and women too, if they wish for a short, easy-to-read, and devotional prayer-book."—*Catholic Opinion*. "A very complete prayer-book. It will be found very useful for children and for travellers."—*Weekly Register*. "A neat little compilation, which will be specially useful to our Catholic School-children. The hymns it contains are some of Fr. Faber's best."—*Universe*.

Devotions for Public and Private Use at the Way of the Cross. By Sister M. F. Clare. Illustrated, 1s.; red edges, 1s. 6d.

Path to Paradise. 36 full page Illustrations. Cloth, 3d. With 50 Illustrations, cloth, 4d.

Manual of Catholic Devotion. 6d.; roan, 1s. 6d.; calf or morocco, 2s. 6d.

S. Patrick's Manual. By the Poor Clares. 4s. 6d.

S. Angela's Manual; a book of devout Prayers and Exercises for Female Youth. *Second edition*. 16mo., cloth, red edges, 2s.; Persian, 3s. 6d.; calf, 4s. 6d.

Crown of Jesus. Persian calf, 6s.; morocco, 7s. 6d. and 8s. 6d., with rims, 10s. 6d.; morocco, extra gilt, 10s. 6d., with rims, 12s. 6d.; ivory, with rims, 21s., 25s., 27s. 6d. and 30s.

Burial of the Dead (Adults and Infants) in Latin and English. Royal 32mo. cloth, 6d.; roan, 1s. 6d.

"Being in a portable form, will be found useful by those who are called upon to assist at that solemn rite."—*Tablet*.

In Suffragiis Sanctorum. Commem S. Josephi. Commem S. Georgii. Set of five for 4d.

Paradise of God; or Virtues of the Sacred Heart. 4s.
Devotions to the Sacred Heart. By the Rev. S. Franco. 4s., paper covers, 2s.
Devotions to the Sacred Heart. By the Rev. J. Joy Dean. Fcap. 8vo. 3s.
Devotions to Sacred Heart of Jesus. By the Rt. Rev. Dr. Milner. *New Edition.* To which is added Devotions to the Immaculate Heart of Mary. 3d.; cloth, 6d.; gilt, 1s.
Sacred Heart of Jesus offered to the Piety of the Young engaged in Study. By Rev. A. Deham, S.J. 6d.
Pleadings of the Sacred Heart. By Rev. P. Comerford. 18mo. 1s.; gilt, 2s.; with the Handbook of the Confraternity, 1s. 6d.; Handbook, separately, 3d.
Treasury of the Sacred Heart. With Epistles and Gospels. 18mo. cloth, 3s. 6d.; roan, 4s. 6d.
Little Treasury of Sacred Heart. 32mo. 2s., roan 2s. 6d. calf or morocco, 5s.
Manual of Devotion to the Sacred Heart, from the Writings of Bl. Margaret Mary Alacoque. By Denys Casassayas. Translated. 3d.
Act of Consecration to the Sacred Heart. 1d.
Act of Reparation to the Sacred Heart. 1s. per 100.
The Little Prayer-Book for Ordinary Catholic Devotions. Cloth, 3d.
Missal (complete). Persian calf, 8s. 6d.; morocco, 10s. 6d., with rims, 13s. 6d.; morocco, extra gilt, 12s. 6d., with rims, 15s. 6d.; morocco, with turn-over edges, 13s. 6d.; morocco antique, 15s.; russia antique, 20s.; ivory, with rims, 31s. 6d.
Catholic Hours: a Manual of Prayer, including Mass and Vespers. By J. R. Digby Beste, Esq. 32mo. cloth, 2s; red edges, 2s. 6d.; roan, 3s.; morocco, 6s.
A Prayer to be said for three days before Holy Communion, and another for three days after. 1d., or 6s. 100.
Ursuline Manual. Persian calf, 7s. 6d.; morocco, 10s.
A New Year's Gift to our Heavenly Father. 4d.

R. Washbourne, 18 Paternoster Row, London.

Manual of Catholic Piety. Edition with green border. French mor., 2s. 6d. ; mor., 4s.

Occasional Prayers for Festivals. By Rev. T. Barge. 32mo. 4d. and 6d. ; gilt, 1s.

Illustrated Manual of Prayers. 32mo. 3d. ; cloth, 4d.

Key of Heaven. Very large type, 1s. Leather 2s. 6d. gilt, 3s.

Catholic Piety. 32mo. 6d. ; roan, 1s. ; with Epistles and Gospels, roan, 1s. ; French morocco, 1s. 6d., with rims and clasp, 2s.; imitation ivory, rims and clasp, 2s. 6d. ; velvet rims and clasps, 3s. 6d.

Key of Heaven. Same size and prices.

Catholic Piety, or Key of Heaven, with Epistles and Gospels. Large 32mo. roan 2s. ; French morocco, with rims, 3s. ; extra gilt, 3s. ; with rims, 3s. 6d.

Novena of Meditations in Honour of S. Joseph, according to the method of S. Ignatius; preceded by a new exercise for hearing Mass according to the intentions of the souls in Purgatory. 18mo. 1s. 6d.

Novena to St. Joseph. Translated by M. A. Macdaniel. To which is added a Pastoral of the late Right Rev. Dr. Grant. 32mo. 4d. ; cloth, 6d.

Devotions for Mass. Very large type, 2d.

Memorare Mass. By the Poor Clares of Kenmare, 2d.

Fourteen Stations of the Holy Way of the Cross. By St. Liguori. Large type edition, 1d.

Indulgences attached to Medals, Crosses, Statues, &c., by the Blessing of His Holiness and of those privileged to give his Blessing. 1s. 2d. per 100, post free.

A Union of our life with the Passion of our Lord by a daily offering. 1s. 2d. per 100, post free.

Prayer for one's Confessor. 1s. 2d. per 100, post free.

Prayer to S. Philip Neri. 1d. each, or 6d. a dozen.

Litany of Resignation. 1s. 2d. per 100, post free.

A Christmas Offering. 1s. a 100, or 7s. 6d. a 1000.

Intentions for Indulgences. 7d. per 100, post free.

Devotions to St. Joseph. 1s. 2d. per 100, post free.

Litany of S. Joseph, &c. 1s. 2d. per 100, post free.

Devotion to St. Joseph as Patron of the Church. 1d.

Catholic Psalmist: or, Manual of Sacred Music, with the Gregorian Chants for High Mass, Holy Week, &c. Compiled by C. B. Lyons, 4s.

The Complete Hymn Book, 136 Hymns. Price 1d.

Douai Bible. 2s. 6d.; Persian calf, 5s.; calf or morocco, 7s.; gilt, 8s. 6d.

Church Hymns. By J. R. Digby Beste, Esq. 6d.

Catholic Choir Manual: Vespers, Hymns and Litanies, &c. Compiled by C. B. Lyons. 1s.

Prayers for the Dying. 1s. 2d. per 100, post free.

Indulgenced Prayer before a Crucifix. 1d. ea., or 6s. 100.

Indulgenced Prayers for Souls in Purgatory. 1s. per 100.

Indulgenced Prayers for the Rosary for the Holy Souls. 1d. each, 6d. a dozen, 3s. per 100.

The Rosary for the Souls in Purgatory, *with Indulgenced Prayer*. 6d., 8d. and 9d. each. Medals separately, 1d. each, 9s. gross.

Rome, &c.

Two Years in the Pontifical Zouaves. By Joseph Powell, Z.P. With 4 Engravings. 8vo. 3s. 6d.

"It affords us much pleasure, and deserves the notice of the Catholic public."—*Tablet*. "Familiar names meet the eye on every page, and as few Catholic circles in either country have not had a friend or relative at one time or another serving in the Pontifical Zouaves, the history of the formation of the corps, of the gallant youths, their sufferings, and their troubles, will be valued as something more than a contribution to modern Roman history."—*Freeman's Journal*.

The Victories of Rome. By Rev. Fr. Beste. 1s.

Rome and her Captors. Letters collected and edited by Count Henri d'Ideville, and translated by F. R. Wegg-Prosser. Cr. 8vo. 4s.

Defence of the Roman Church against Fr. Gratry. By Dom Gueranger. 1s. 6d.

Personal Recollections of Rome. By W. J. Jacob, Esq., late of the Pontifical Zouaves. 8vo. 1s. 6d.

Supremacy of the Roman See. By C. E. Tame. 6d.

The Roman Question. By F. C. Husenbeth, D.D. 6d.

Henri V. (Comte de Chambord), September 29, 1873. By W. H. Walsh. With a Portrait. 8vo. 1s. 6d.

The Rule of the Pope-King. By Rev. Fr. Martin. 6d.

The Years of Peter. By an Ex-Papal Zouave. 1d.
The Catechism of the Council. By a D.C.L. 2d.
Civilization and the See of Rome. By Lord Robert Montagu, M.P. 6d.
Rome, semper eadem. By Denis Patrick Michael O'Mahony. 1s. 6d.
A Few Remarks on a pamphlet entitled the "Divine Decrees." 6d.

Tales, or Books for the Library.

Tom's Crucifix, and other Tales. By M. F. S. 3s.
"Eight simple stories for the use of teachers of Christian doctrine."—*Universe*. "This is a volume of short, plain, and simple stories, written with the view of illustrating the Catholic religion practically by putting Catholic practices in an interesting light before the mental eyes of children....The whole of the tales in the volume before us are exceedingly well written."—*Register*.

Simple Tales. Square 16mo. cloth antique, 2s. 6d.
"Contains five pretty stories of a true Catholic tone, interspersed with some short pieces of poetry. . . Are very affecting, and told in such a way as to engage the attention of any child."—*Register*. "This is a little book which we can recommend with great confidence. The tales are simple, beautiful, and pathetic."—*Catholic Opinion*. "It belongs to a class of books of which the want is generally much felt by Catholic parents."—*Dublin Review*. "Beautifully written. 'Little Terence' is a gem of a Tale."—*Tablet*.

Terry O'Flinn's Examination of Conscience. By the Very Rev. Dr. Tandy. Fcap. 8vo. 1s. 6d.; extra gilt, 2s.; cheap edition, 1s.
"The writer possesses considerable literary power."—*Register*.

The Adventures of a Protestant in Search of a Religion: being the Story of a late Student of Divinity at Bunyan Baptist College; a Nonconformist Minister, who seceded to the Catholic Church. By Iota. 5s.; cheap edition, 3s.
"Will well repay its perusal."—*Universe*. "This precious volume."—*Baptist*. "No one will deny 'Iota' the merit of entire originality."—*Civilian*. "A valuable addition to every Catholic library." *Tablet*. "There is much cleverness in it."—*Nonconformist*. "Malicious and wicked."—*English Independent*.

The People's Martyr, a Legend of Canterbury. 4s.
Rupert Aubray. By the Rev. T. J. Potter. 3s.
Farleyes of Farleye. By the same author. 2s. 6d.
Sir Humphrey's Trial. By the same author. 2s. 6d.

A Wasted Life. By Rosa Baughan. 8vo. 3s. 6d.
The Village Lily. Fcap. 8vo. 1s.; gilt, 1s. 6d.
Fairy Tales for Little Children. By Madeleine Howley Meehan. Fcap. 1s.; cloth extra, 1s. 6d.; gilt, 2s.

"Full of imagination and dreams, and at the same time with excellent point and practical aim, within the reach of the intelligence of infants."—*Universe.* "Pleasing, simple stories, combining instruction with amusement."—*Register.*

Rosalie; or, the Memoirs of a French Child. Written by herself. Fcap. 8vo., 1s. and 1s. 6d.; extra gilt, 2s.

"It is prettily told, and in a natural manner. The account of Rosalie's illness and First Communion is very well related. We can recommend the book for the reading of children."—*Tablet.* "The tenth chapter is beautiful."—*Universe.*

The Story of Marie and other Tales. Fcap. 8vo., 2s.; cloth extra, 2s. 6d.; gilt, 3s.; or separately:—The Story of Marie, 2d.; Nelly Blane, and A Contrast, 2d.; A Conversion and a Death-Bed, 2d.; Herbert Montagu, 2d.; Jane Murphy, The Dying Gipsy, and The Nameless Grave, 2d.; The Beggars, and True and False Riches, 2d.; Pat and his Friend, 2d.

"A very nice little collection of stories, thoroughly Catholic in their teaching."—*Tablet.* "A series of short pretty stories, told with much simplicity."—*Universe.* "A number of short pretty stories, replete with religious teaching, told in simple language."—*Weekly Register.*

The Last of the Catholic O'Malleys. A Tale. By M. Taunton. 18mo. cloth, 1s. 6d.; extra, 2s.

"A sad and stirring tale, simply written, and sure to secure for itself readers."—*Tablet.* "Deeply interesting. It is well adapted for parochial and school libraries."—*Weekly Register.* "A very pleasing tale."—*The Month.*

Eagle and Dove. From the French of Mademoiselle Zénaïde Fleuriot. By Emily Bowles. Cr. 8vo., 5s.

"We recommend our readers to peruse this well-written story."—*Register.* "One of the very best stories we have ever dipped into."—*Church Times.* "Admirable in tone and purpose."—*Church Herald.* "A real gain. It possesses merits far above the pretty fictions got up by English writers."—*Dublin Review.* "There is an air of truth and sobriety about this little volume, nor is there any attempt at sensation."—*Tablet.*

Cistercian Legends of the 13th Century. Translated from the Latin by the Rev. Henry Collins. 3s.
Cloister Legends: or, Convents and Monasteries in the Olden Time. *Second Edition.* Cr. 8vo. 4s.

R. Washbourne, 18 *Paternoster Row, London.*

Chats about the Rosary; or, Aunt Margaret's Little Neighbours. Fcap. 8vo. 3s.

"There is scarcely any devotion so calculated as the Rosary to keep up a taste for piety in little children, and we must be grateful for any help in applying its lessons to the daily life of those who already love it in their unconscious tribute to its value and beauty."—*Month.* "We do not know of a better book for reading aloud to children, it will teach them to understand and to love the Rosary."—*Tablet.* "A graceful little book, in fifteen chapters, on the Rosary, illustrative of each of the mysteries, and connecting each with the practice of some particular virtue."—*Catholic Opinion.*

Margarethe Verflassen. Translated from the German by Mrs. Smith Sligo. Fcap. 8vo. 3s.; gilt, 3s. 6d.

"A portrait of a very holy and noble soul, whose life was passed in constant practical acts of the love of God."—*Weekly Register.* "It is the picture of a true woman's life, well fitted up with the practice of ascetic devotion and loving unwearied activity about all the works of mercy."—*Tablet.*

Keighley Hall and other Tales. By Elizabeth King. 18mo. 6d.; cloth, 1s.; gilt, 1s. 6d.; or, separately, Keighley Hall, Clouds and Sunshine, The Maltese Cross, 3d. each.

Sir Ælfric and other Tales. By the Rev. G. Bampfield. 18mo. 6d.; cloth, 1s.; gilt, 1s. 6d.

Ned Rusheen. By the Poor Clares. Crown 8vo. 6s.

The Prussian Spy. A Novel. By V. Valmont. 4s.

Adolphus; or, the Good Son. 18mo. gilt, 6d.

Nicholas; or, the Reward of a Good Action. 6d.

The Lost Children of Mount St. Bernard. 18mo. gilt, 6d.

The Baker's Boy; or, the Results of Industry. 6d.

A Broken Chain. 18mo. gilt, 6d.

"All prettily got up, artistically illustrated, and pleasantly-written. Better books for gifts and rewards we do not know."—*Weekly Register.* "We can thoroughly recommend them."—*Tablet.*

The Truce of God: a Tale of the Eleventh Century. By G. H. Miles. 4s.

Tales and Sketches. By Charles Fleet. 8vo. cloth, 2s. and 2s. 6d.; cloth, gilt, 3s. 6d.

The Artist of Collingwood. By Baron Na Carriag. 3s. 6d.

The Convent Prize Book. By the author of "Geraldine." Fcap. 8vo. 2s. 6d.; gilt, 3s. 6d.

R. Washbourne, 18 Paternoster Row, London.

Catherine Hamilton. By the author of "Tom's Crucifix," &c. Fcap. 8vo. 2s. 6d. ; gilt, 3s.

Sir Thomas Maxwell and his Ward. By Miss Bridges. Fcap. 8vo. 2s.

Forty Years of American Life. By T. L. Nichols, M.D. 5s.

Catherine grown Older: a sequel to "Catherine Hamilton." Fcap. 8vo. 2s. 6d.; gilt 3s.

Canon Schmid's Tales, selected from his works. A new translation, with 6 original Illustrations. Fcap. 8vo. 3s. 6d.

The Journey of Sophia and Eulalie to the Palace of True Happiness. Translated by the Rev. Father Bradbury, Mount St. Bernard's. Fcap. 8vo. 3s. 6d.; cheap edition, 2s. 6d.

The Fisherman's Daughter. By Conscience. 4s.

The Amulet. By Hendrick Conscience. 4s.

Count Hugo of Graenhove. By Conscience. 4s.

The Village Innkeeper. By Conscience. 4s.

Happiness of being Rich. By Conscience. 4s.

Margaret Roper. By A. M. Stewart. 6s., gilt, 7s.

Florence O'Neill. By A. M. Stewart. 5s. and 6s.

Limerick Veteran. By the same. 5s. and 6s.

The Three Elizabeths. By the same. 5s. and 6s.

Alone in the World. By the same. 3s. 6d. and 4s. 6d.

Festival Tales. By J. F. Waller. 5s.

Shakespeare's Plays and Tragedies. Abridged and Revised for the use of Schools. 8vo. 7s. 6d.

Poems. By H. N. Oxenham. *Third Edition.* 3s. 6d.

Culpepper. An entirely New Edition of Brook's Family Herbal. Cr. 8vo., 150 engravings, 3s. 6d.; drawn and coloured from living specimens. 5s. 6d.

The Catholic Alphabet of Scripture Subjects. Price, on a sheet, plain, 1s.; coloured, 2s.; mounted on linen, to fold in a case, 3s. 6d.; varnished, on linen, on rollers, 4s.

Bell's Modern Reader and Speaker. Cloth, 3s. 6d.

Cogery's Third French Course, with Vocabulary. 2s.

R. Washbourne, 18 *Paternoster Row, London.*

Educational and Miscellaneous.

Horace. Literally translated by Smart. 2s.
Virgil. Literally translated by Davidson. 2s. 6d.
History of Modern Europe. With a Preface by the Right Rev. Dr. Weathers. 12mo. cloth, 5s.; gilt, 6s.; roan, 5s. 6d.

"A work of special importance for the way in which it deals with the early part of the present Pontificate."—*Weekly Register.*

Biographical Readings. By A. M. Stewart. 4s. 6d.
General Questions in History, Chronology, Geography, the Arts, &c. By A. M. Stewart. 4s. 6d.
University Education, under the Guidance of the Church; or, Monastic Studies. By a Monk of St. Augustine's, Ramsgate. 8vo. 2s. 6d.
Elements of Philosophy, comprising Logic, and General Principles of Metaphysics. By Rev. W. H. Hill, S.J. Second edition, 8vo. 6s.
History of England. By W. Mylius. 12mo. 3s. 6d.
Catechism of the History of England. Cloth, 1s.
History of Ireland. By T. Young. 18mo. cloth, 2s. 6d.
The Illustrated History of Ireland. By the Nun of Kenmare. Illustrated by Doyle. 8vo. 11s.
The Patriots' History of Ireland. By the Poor Clares of Kenmare. 18mo. cloth, 2s.; cloth gilt, 2s. 6d.
A Chronological Sketch of the Kings of England and France. With Anecdotes for the use of Children. By H. Murray Lane. 2s. 6d,; or separately, England, 1s. 6d., France, 1s. 6d.

"Admirably adapted for teaching young children the elements of English and French history."—*Tablet.* "A very useful little publication."—*Weekly Register.* "An admirably arranged little work for the use of children."—*Universe.*

Extracts from the Fathers and other Writers of the Church. 12mo. cloth, 4s. 6d.
Brickley's Standard Table Book, ½d.
Washbourne's Multiplication Table on a sheet, . 3s. per 100. Specimen sent for 1d. stamp.

R. Washbourne, 18 Paternoster Row, London.

Music (*Net*).

BY HERR WILHELM SCHULTHES.

Veni Domine. Motett for Four Voices. 2s.; vocal arrangement, 6d.

Cor Jesu, Salus in Te Sperantium. 2s.; with harp accompaniment, 2s. 6d.; abridged edition, 3d.

Mass of the Holy Child Jesus, and Ave Maria for unison and congregational singing, with organ accompaniment. 3s.
  The Vocal Part. 4d.; or in cloth, 6d.

The Ave Maria of this Mass can be had for Four Voices, with the Ingressus Angelus. 1s. 3d.

Recordare. Oratio Jeremiæ Prophetæ. 1s.

Ne projicias me a facie Tua. Motett for Four Voices. (T.B.) 1s. 3d.

Benediction Service, with 36 Litanies. 6s.

Oratory Hymns. 2 vols., 8s.

Regina Cœli. Motett for Four Voices. 3s.; vocal arrangement, 1s.

Twelve Latin Hymns, for Vespers, &c. 2s.

Litanies. By Rev. J. McCarthy. 1s. 3d.
Six Litany Chants. By F. Leslie. 6d.
Ave Maria. By T. Haydn Waud. 1s. 6d.
Fr. Faber's Hymns. Various, 9d. each.
Portfolio. With a patent metallic back. 3s.

A separate Catalogue of FOREIGN Books, Educational Books, Books for the Library or for Prizes, supplied; also a Catalogue of School and General Stationery, a Catalogue of Secondhand Books, and a Catalogue of Crucifixes and other Religious Articles.

INDEX TO AUTHORS.

	PAGE		PAGE
Arnold, Miss M. J.	3	Laing, Rev. Dr.	14, 16, 21
A'Kempis, Thomas	9	Lambilotte, Rev. Père	7
Allies, T. W., Esq.	11	Lane, H. Murray, Esq.	30
Amherst, Bishop	9	M'Corry, Rev. Dr.	17
Bagshawe, Rev. J. B.	15	Macdaniel, Miss	3, 21, 24
Bampfield, Rev. G.	28	Macleod, Rev. X. D.	21
Barge, Rev. T.	24	Manning, Most Rev. Dr.	2, 14, 19
Beste, J. R. D., Esq.	11, 23, 25	Marshall, T. W. M., Esq.	11
Beste, Rev. K. D.	25	Meehan, Madeleine Howley	27
Bethell, Rev. A. P.	20	Mermillod, Mgr.	8
Blosius	8	Milner, Bishop	23
Bona, Cardinal	2	M. F. S.	2, 3, 18, 26
Boudon, Mgr.	8	Nary, Rev. J.	15
Bowles, Emily	27	Newman, Dr.	4
Bradbury, Rev. Fr.	29	O'Clery, Chevalier	3
Browne, E. G. K.	14	O'Mahony, D. P. M.	26
Brownlow, Rev. W. R. B.	6, 13	Oratorian Lives of the Saints	18
Burder, Rt. Rev. Abbot	7	Oxenham, H. N.	12, 29
Burke, S. H., M.A.	13	Ozanam, Professor	4
Butler, Alban	9, 17	Philpin, Rev. Fr.	7
Challoner, Bishop	16	Platus, Fr. Jerome	17
Collins, Rev. Fr.	10	Poirier, Bishop	15
Compton, Herbert	2	Poor Clares	13, 20, 22
Dechamps, Mgr.	11	Powell, J., Esq.	25
Deham, Rev. A.	23	Pye, H. J., Esq.	16
Dixon, Rev. Fr.	3	Ravignan, Père	8
Doyotte, Rev. Père	2	Redmond, Rev. Dr.	13
Dupanloup, Mgr.	4	Richardson, Rev. Fr.	17
Francis of Sales, St.	11, 12	Robinson, W. C.	4
Frassinetti	16	Schulthes, Herr	31
Gibson, Rev. H.	15	Shakespeare	29
Grace Ramsay	19	Shepard, T. S., Esq.	19
Grant, Bishop	24	Sligo, A. V. Smith, Esq.	17
Gueranger	25	Sligo, Mrs. Smith	28
Hedley, Bishop	8	Stewart, A. M.	29, 30
Henry, Lucien	7	Tame, C. E., Esq.	21, 25
Herbert, Lady	3, 7, 18	Tandy, Very Rev. Dr.	26
Hill, Rev. Fr.	30	Taunton, Mrs.	27
Hope, Mrs.	9	Tondini, Rev. C.	4, 5
Husenbeth, Dr.	4, 6, 20, 21	Wegg-Prosser, F. R.	25
Kenny, Dr.	17	Williams, Canon	17
King, Miss	28		

CONTENTS.

	PAGE		PAGE
New Books	1	Prayer-Books	22
Dramas, Comedies, Farces	4	Rome, &c.	25
Religious Reading	6	Tales, or Books for Library	26
Religious Instruction	15	Educational Works	30
Lives of Saints, &c.	17	Music	31
Our Lady, Works relating to	20		

R. WASHBOURNE, 18 PATERNOSTER ROW.

www.ingramcontent.com/pod-product-compliance
Lightning Source LLC
Chambersburg PA
CBHW031949230426
43672CB00010B/2099